FROM FEAR TO FLOURISH

Female Entrepreneurs Unleashing Their Inner Badass For *Unstoppable Success*

Amanda Brenkley In Collaboration

© Copyright – Amanda Brenkley 2024
By Pro Publishing House

ISBN: 9798879260717

The following chapters are Amanda Brenkley's intellectual property and the stories of the individuals. All rights reserved. No part of this book may be reproduced or modified in any form, including photocopying, recording, or by information storage and retrieval system, without written permission from the publisher/author.
All rights reserved.

Legal Notice:

This book is for personal use only. You cannot amend, distribute, sell, use, quote or paraphrase any part of this book's content without the author's or copyright owner's consent. Legal action will be pursued if this is breached. The information provided herein is stated to be truthful and consistent in that any liability, in terms of inattention or otherwise, by any usage or abuse of any policies, processes, or directions contained within is the solitary and utter responsibility of the recipient reader. Under no circumstances will any legal responsibility or blame be held against the publisher for any reparation, damages, or monetary loss due to the information herein, either directly or indirectly.

Disclaimer Notice:

Amanda is not a doctor or providing medical recommendations; this book is not providing medical advice; it is intended for informational purposes only. It is not a substitute for professional medical advice, diagnosis or treatment. Never ignore professional medical advice in seeking treatment. Every attempt has been made to provide accurate, up-to-date, reliable, and complete information. No warranties of any kind are expressed or implied. Readers acknowledge that the author is not engaging in the rendering of legal, financial, medical or professional advice.

By reading this document, the reader agrees that under no circumstances are we responsible for any losses, direct or indirect, which are incurred as a result of the use of the information contained within this document, including, but not limited to, — errors, omissions, or inaccuracies.

Amanda has tried to ensure that the weblinks and references are correct and active at the time of publishing. However, Amanda cannot guarantee this and takes no responsibility for the websites remaining live or that the content will remain relevant.

Book Cover Design: Tracey Munro
Book Cover Illustration: Ella Munro

DEDICATION

With profound gratitude and boundless love, I dedicate this book to the extraordinary souls who have shaped my journey. Foremost among them are the remarkable women who, with unwavering courage, joined forces in the collaborative creation of this book. They dared greatly, baring their souls to share stories and insights with a vulnerability that is both awe-inspiring and empowering.

In a world that often encourages silence, these amazing women stood tall, embracing the challenge to be seen and heard. Their willingness to open up so openly and honestly is a testament to the strength that resides within, a strength that transcends the boundaries of fear and self-doubt. To collaborate is to dance on the delicate edge of vulnerability, and I am profoundly grateful to these women for their bravery. Each page of this book carries the echoes of their resilience, wisdom, and the beauty that emerges when authenticity takes centre stage.

To my dearest Mum—your unwavering belief in my potential was the guiding light that led me to embark on the path of creating a life and business that fills me with pride. Your persistent encouragement echoes in my heart, and I am eternally thankful for your steadfast support. Though you may no longer tread this earthly realm, your spirit resides within me, a timeless presence that fuels my endeavours. Thank you for instilling in me the confidence to overcome self-doubt and for envisioning a world of limitless possibilities. Your love lives on, an enduring force that propels me forward.

To my cherished boys, Jamo and Kenzo—you are the heartbeat of my existence, the source of immeasurable pride and inspiration. I dedicate this work to you both as " I love you big much" a love that knows no bounds. Your presence in my life has fuelled my determination to strive for excellence. My deepest desire for you is to embrace happiness, forge a life you passionately love, and recognise that the only limitations that exist are the ones we impose upon ourselves. Dream audaciously, my beloved sons, and relentlessly pursue the actions that will craft the life you truly deserve.

May this book stand as a testament to the profound impact you've had on my journey, and may its pages echo the resounding gratitude and love that fill my heart.

CONTENTS

INTRODUCTION — Page:7

FORWARD — Page:9

CHAPTER 1: Amanda Brenkley — Page:13

  PART 1: Fear Unleashed: — Page:25
Conquering Fear and Anxiety to Ignite Success

  PART 2: Mindshift Mastery: — Page:37
Reflecting on the Power of a Flourishing Mindset

  PART 3: Boundaries of Brilliance: — Page:45
Goal setting for Fearless Triumph

  PART 4: Self-Care Symphony: — Page:49
Nurturing the Entrepreneurial Soul

  PART 5: Strategic Brilliance: — Page:57
Mastering the Art of Fearless Execution

  PART 6: Halt the Hesitation: — Page:63
Breaking Free from the Chains of Doubt

CHAPTER 2: Loretta Jeffery — Page:69

CHAPTER 3: Terri Brown — Page:79

CHAPTER 4: Shevanne Helmer　　　　　　　Page:89

CHAPTER 5: Lucy Paterson　　　　　　　　Page:101

CHAPTER 6: Laura Crosby　　　　　　　　Page:111

CHAPTER 7: Annemarie Farrow　　　　　　Page:121

CHAPTER 8: Julie Hollins　　　　　　　　　Page:131

CHAPTER 9: Aisha Beg　　　　　　　　　　Page:141

CHAPTER 10: Suzanne Robinson　　　　　Page:159

CHAPTER 11: Jacky Allan　　　　　　　　Page:167

CHAPTER 12: Michelle Wynne　　　　　　Page:175

CHAPTER 13: Sally Tarbox　　　　　　　　Page:185

CHAPTER 14: Lara Lee Caine　　　　　　　Page:195

CHAPTER 15: Beverley Storey　　　　　　Page:205

CHAPTER 16: Andrea Rainsford　　　　　　Page:215

CHAPTER 17: Abbi Titley　　　　　　　　Page:225

CHAPTER 18: Sarah Knight　　　　　　　Page: 237

CHAPTER 19: Sandra Fletcher　　　　　　Page: 247

ACKNOWLEGEMENTS　　　　　　　　Page:255

INTRODUCTION

You may have picked up this book because you know you are meant for more. So, buckle up and prepare to embark on a transformative journey. This book is designed to empower you in embracing change and fostering growth. If you've ever felt the weight of difficulty while navigating the path of change, know this: the challenge lies not in your efforts but in the inherent nature of change itself. Fear not, for this guide is your ally, offering the support and guidance needed to make the seemingly arduous journey more accessible.

Should you encounter a sense of discomfort as you delve into these pages, recognise it as the subtle resistance and self-sabotage that often accompany personal evolution. It's entirely natural to feel this resistance when striving to reshape your mindset and elevate your business endeavours.

Approach this book with an open mind and heart, ready to explore new perspectives and engage with the transformative reflective questions provided. Within these pages lie the breakthrough moments that promise a profound shift in mindset and business strategy.

The reflective questions presented here are powerful tools meant to amplify your self-discovery. Embrace them with honesty and authenticity, responding instinctively before your conscious mind has a chance to intervene with doubt.

Don't underestimate the significance of this introspective process; it is the crucible in which a resilient growth mindset is forged—the very mindset proven to dismantle the shackles of perfectionism and the fear of failure, impediments that often hinder one's journey to reaching their full potential.

Throughout your reading, I encourage you to take notes. Writing, as proven by research, accelerates self-awareness and self-management. By documenting your insights and actions, you not only enhance your understanding but also solidify your commitment to turning aspirations into tangible realities.

Your journey to overcoming obstacles, unlocking potential, and embracing change begins here. May these words guide you towards the profound shifts that await on the horizon of your personal and professional growth in life and business.

FORWORD
Amanda Brenkley

Welcome to the empowering world of "From Fear to Flourish," a compelling odyssey through the inspiring stories of resilient women entrepreneurs who have transcended their fears to achieve unparalleled success. I am Amanda Brenkley, your coach on this transformative journey, and it is with great excitement that I invite you to delve into the pages that unfold the secrets of their triumphs.

In the fast-paced landscape of contemporary business, we find ourselves at an unprecedented juncture – a time of limitless opportunities and boundless potential. "From Fear to Flourish" serves as a beacon for those with an entrepreneurial spirit, seeking not only success but a life filled with purpose, passion, and prosperity. As a coach, therapist, and the founder of the Coaching Mastery Academy, I've had the privilege of witnessing the indomitable spirit of countless women who have fearlessly ventured into the world of entrepreneurship.

This book is more than a compilation of success stories; it's a comprehensive guide that encapsulates the strategies, challenges, and triumphs of extraordinary women who have dared to dream big and achieve even bigger. Throughout these pages, we will unravel the intricacies of their journeys, exploring the highs and lows, the moments of triumph, and the hurdles that seemed insurmountable. The stories you're about to encounter are not just stories – they are blueprints, offering you insights and tools to navigate your unique path to success.

Each woman featured in "From Fear to Flourish" has generously shared not only her achievements but also her vulnerabilities, doubts, and the pivotal moments that defined her journey. It's a collective narrative that reveals the human side of entrepreneurship, dispelling the myth that success is a linear path devoid of challenges. Be prepared to witness the good, the bad, and the ugly, for it is within these raw and authentic stories that you'll find the fuel to propel yourself forward in your life and business.

As you embark on this enriching expedition, envision this book not merely as a literary piece but as a mentor, a confidante, and a trusted guide. The strategies laid out within these pages are not theoretical concepts but tried-and-true methods that these women have employed to overcome obstacles and flourish in their respective domains. The women you are about to meet are not just entrepreneurs; they are visionaries, trailblazers, and beacons of inspiration. They have faced challenges head-on, embraced vulnerability as a source of strength, and cultivated resilience that has become the cornerstone of their success.

This book is a celebration of their bravery, a salute to their unwavering commitment, and a testament to the limitless possibilities that await those who dare to dream and take action. Allow me to guide you through the narrative tapestry of "From Fear to Flourish." Each chapter unfolds a new story, a fresh perspective, and lessons that extend far beyond **the realm of business.**

These are stories of transformation, of turning fear into a catalyst for growth, and of flourishing in both the professional and personal spheres. In the ensuing chapters, you will encounter the stories of women who have navigated the complexities of entrepreneurship with grace, resilience, and an unwavering belief in their vision. These are women who have transcended societal norms, shattered glass ceilings, and emerged as leaders in their respective fields. Their journeys are diverse, and yet, the common thread is the courage to face fear and transform it into a stepping stone toward success.

You may find yourself resonating with the challenges they've faced – the self-doubt, the naysayers, the financial struggles, and the moments of uncertainty. Yet, within these stories, you will discover the strategies, mindset shifts, and actionable steps that propelled them forward. It is my hope that you draw inspiration from their experiences, finding solace in the shared struggles and motivation in the shared victories.

As you flip through these pages, you'll encounter real women with real stories, and it's my sincere belief that you will recognise parts of yourself in their narratives. Whether you are an aspiring entrepreneur, a seasoned business owner, or you're someone contemplating taking the leap into entrepreneurship, there is something here for you. Consider this book a roadmap, a mentorship program, and a source of empowerment that extends beyond the confines of its pages. So, buckle up for a journey that transcends fear, embraces vulnerability, and culminates in unparalleled success. "From Fear to Flourish" is not just a book; it's a movement, an affirmation that success is within reach for those who are willing to confront their fears and embark on the path less travelled.

Amanda Brenkley
Author, Coach, Therapist and Trainer
Founder and CEO of the Coaching Mastery Academy
As seen on Fox TV and Cosmopolitan and Authority magazine

Linktree: www.linktr.ee/amandabrenkley37

CHAPTER 1

Amanda Brenkley

Social Worker, Coach, Therapist, Author, Motivational Speaker, and Trainer

Breaking Through Barriers - From Fear to Flourish a Journey of Unapologetic Growth

In this extended exploration of my life's journey, I invite you to delve deeper into the intricate tapestry of my experiences, challenges, and triumphs. I never dreamt that I would become an entrepreneur, but where focus goes, energy flows. My resume, though impressive now, emerges as a testament to resilience, continuous learning, and the absolute audacity to dream big! Let's unravel the layers of my story, exposing the rawness of my past, the transformative power of tragedy, and the rebirth into a life I now cherish.

The Struggles of School and the Birth of Limiting Beliefs

The notion that "school is the best days of your life" always seemed like a distant mirage for me as it never resonated with me. Instead, my school years felt like navigating a labyrinth of challenges, each turn more daunting than the last. My school was in England and situated in a town which was listed as one of the government's most deprived areas. I grappled with deep-seated self-confidence issues, amplified by periods of bullying that seemed to follow me like a shadow. The environment was stifling, characterised by uninspiring teaching methods and an oppressive atmosphere that did little to nurture my spirit or intellect.

At the heart of my struggles was an undiagnosed condition that silently shaped my academic and social experiences: dyslexia. This learning difficulty, masked and unacknowledged, significantly influenced my perception of myself. I frequently found myself battling the crippling belief that I was "thick" and "stupid," labels that seemed to stick despite my best efforts. These perceptions were not just self-imposed; they were often echoed by those around me, further entrenching my sense of inadequacy because I heard this enough that I adopted the belief that this must be my reality; I must be stupid. All our thoughts, words, beliefs, and habits provide a blueprint for our minds and bodies.

My shyness was not just a trait but a defence mechanism. I was a child with a processing delay, one who often let others speak on my behalf because it felt safer and easier. Looking back, it's clear that my voice was lost amidst the cacophony of louder, more confident voices. This silence was not only a shield against the academic challenges but also a cloak hiding deeper, more painful truths.

The home that should have always been my sanctuary was instead, at times, a theatre of silent torment. Although I have many fond, happy childhood memories, and I am grateful to my parents, who did their very best, they have loved me dearly and gave me everything they could. My home featured at times, the presence of domestic abuse, alcohol misuse and mental health difficulties, which is a toxic combination that can have a detrimental impact on a child's development. Consequently, at times, this was a reality too harsh for me to bear but was part of my existence. I became a keeper of secrets, not just my own but those of my family. The weight of these secrets was a constant burden, yet I bore them silently, fearing the consequences their revelation might bring upon those involved.

During these formative years, my identity was being moulded by a mix of external perceptions and internal fears. The intersection of my learning difficulties and the unpredictability of my home life created a complex tapestry of emotional and cognitive challenges. I navigated through each day carrying a heavy load of unresolved emotions and unspoken truths.

These experiences, though on a few occasions were harrowing, were the crucibles that forged my resilience. They were the silent tutors who taught me empathy, the unseen forces that pushed me towards a path of healing and helping others. My journey through these early years laid the groundwork for the person I would become – a person who, despite the odds, chose to rise above the circumstances and rewrite her narrative. I was keen to be the best version of myself, the best mother I could be, and to make a difference to those who feel stuck. I recognised that to be the best version of myself, I needed to grow and contribute to others, and this is where I learned that fulfilment lies.

It is in the reflection of these years that I find a profound understanding of my journey. The pain, the struggles, and the silent battles were not in vain. They were the seeds from which my future self would grow – a self that learned to find her voice, stand in her truth, and ultimately, help others do the same.

"I do not doubt that my childhood experiences and limiting beliefs held me back at school," I admit, acknowledging the formidable impact of those early struggles. My journey towards education, surprisingly, commenced after school and started predominantly when I attended college which provided the supportive environment I needed. The incredible tutors and a newfound sense of belonging propelled me forward. It was here that I discovered my potential, setting the stage for a transformative fourteen-year journey in higher education. I then went on to successfully gain three degrees from Staffordshire University, two of which I studied at the same time. This was something I was told was impossible and had never been done before, and they tried to put me off from doing it, but I was immensely proud to be the first person ever to be awarded two degrees in the same year.

Whilst this was many years ago, I am still awaiting my special achievement award from Staffordshire. The girl whose name was stupid eventually learned she was not. From there, I gained post-qualifying studies from Keele University; I have also been a practice Educator for Keele University, assessing and supporting social work students. This is something I am immensely proud to have accomplished as I am an advocate for lifelong learning, and I will always be invested in the interface of social work.

Navigating Tragedy: A Pivotal Moment in 2009

The year 2009 marked a turning point in my life, a moment etched in memory with the sharpness of grief. It was during a camping holiday, not far from home, when the unimaginable happened – the sudden and tragic passing of my mum, Paula. The news came like a bolt from the blue, shattering the serenity of our vacation and plunging me into a whirlwind of sorrow.

The emotional landscape of my world changed drastically in that instance. "You never expect to lose people in this way," I reflect, still feeling the raw intensity of those emotions. The impact of her departure was profound, leaving a permanent imprint on my soul. This was more than just a loss; it was a crucible of my endurance, a moment that demanded every ounce of strength I had, fuelled by the boundless love for my children and family; this was my saving grace.

In the aftermath of this tragedy, a shadow of fear began to cloud my life. I developed a fear of happiness, an apprehension of enduring another loss. Subconsciously, I began to curb my joy, as if by limiting my happiness, I could somehow shield myself from future pain. This mindset, a direct consequence of my trauma, held me captive for nearly a decade, stunting my personal growth and dimming the vibrancy of my personality. "I felt like my personality had gone bland," I admit, acknowledging the period of emotional self-harm and the pervasive dullness that defined those years. The support from my family during this time was my lifeline – their solidarity and mutual support became the foundation on which we collectively began to heal.

Grieving for my mum was a journey through a landscape filled with complex emotions. It wasn't a single feeling but a tumultuous mix of loss, fear, and identity crisis. I was in a state of acute grief, struggling to navigate not just my own emotions but also guiding my children towards a healthier emotional state. This phase was undoubtedly the darkest period of my life, I was surviving and not thriving, it was marked by an overwhelming sense of powerlessness. The realisation that I could do nothing to reverse or change what had happened was a profound source of anguish.

Grief, I learned, is not a straightforward path. It meanders through various emotions, sometimes hitting you with the force of a tidal wave, other times creeping in quietly. In grappling with these feelings, I began to understand the multifaceted nature of grief and the importance of allowing oneself to fully experience and process these emotions.

Through this harrowing journey, I emerged with a deeper understanding of life's fragility and the strength that lies in vulnerability. My experience with grief, as heart-wrenching as it was, became a pivotal chapter in my life, teaching me invaluable lessons about love, loss, resilience, and the indomitable spirit of the human heart. I lay bare the profound impact of personal tragedy and the complex journey of navigating grief. I feel it has a place in conversation, as it's a reflection on the resilience of the human spirit in the face of unimaginable loss and a testament to the power of family, love, and inner strength in overcoming the darkest hours of our lives.

Global Ventures: Living and Learning from Country to Country

As I journeyed through the labyrinth of my academic and personal growth, an insatiable passion for travel and cultural diversity took root within me. This yearning for exploration was not sudden; it was a flame gently fanned by the cherished memories of childhood holidays in Spain and the captivating tales of global travels and entrepreneurship shared by my grandad, Martin, who has been my rock and inspiration to drive me to do better.

At the tender age of 19, armed with dreams larger than my suitcase, I took a bold step beyond the familiar. I ventured to Holland, a decision fuelled by an innate desire to escape the monotony of a predictable 9-5 life. This was more than a mere change of scenery; it was a quest for a deeper understanding of myself and the world around me. Holland was an eye-opener, and I loved the country for all its culture and the expectational kind people who resided there, I explored and learnt a lot, but it was Spain that captured a piece of my heart, transforming from a holiday destination to a second home. The warm Mediterranean sun, the vibrant culture, and the spirited people provided a stark contrast to the life I had known. I lived in Menorca for some time, residing across from the beach. The ocean there held a special allure for me; its presence was rejuvenating, filling me with energy whenever I was near.

Reflecting on those family holidays to Spain, I can't help but smile. "These were some of my greatest experiences," I fondly recall. The Spanish sojourns were not just vacations; they were rare havens of joy and safety, a precious time when life's regular tumults seemed to pause, allowing me to truly relax and imbibe the essence of living. We shared these experiences often with great friends, and I am so grateful we had the opportunity to experience travel at such a young age, again thanks to my grandad and his endeavours as we would stay in my grandparent's villa, giving us the opportunities, which may not have been available to us otherwise.

However, nestled within me was a dream that was yet to take flight – a dream about a land down under, Australia. This dream, which persisted through years of life's twists and turns, started as my uncle Clive had been a ten-pound pom, and whilst we never had the opportunity to visit when I was a child, my cousins would come to England and tell us how good it was. Everything I watched on TV was Australia from Home and Away, Neighbours, to Wanted Down Under and Bondi Rescue. In reflection, I guess it was inevitable that my obsession with Australia would become my children's obsession as their world was surrounded by the dream of Down Under.

One day, I decided to make a vision board with my children, I wanted them to recognise the power of the law of attraction. We printed off pictures, and they put on a photo of Australia and declared this is where we want to live. I recall there was a picture of a kangaroo and a koala. Admittedly, I did go to bed that night concerned, and I was worried I had set them up to fail. I had said to them that anything they put on the board is likely to come true if they set an intention. However, I expected a trip to Alton Towers, maybe a holiday to Disney. But no, they had been bred to think big, I should have known better. Anyway, a few weeks later, a dear friend of mine, Peter called me to say he had an interview for a social work job in Melbourne, he said it was informal information gathering mainly and would I like to go. I will confess initially, I said no. I was confused. We had not worked together for over five years, so why would he think of me? Why would he call out of the blue? Eventually, I texted him back and said yes, why not? There is no harm in learning more. I considered this was the universe working to conspire, bringing about the very intention the boys had set in that vision board.

Less than a year later, Australia finally took shape in 2018. The decision to move to Australia was monumental, especially as a single parent with two teenage boys. It was a leap not just across continents but into a realm of unknowns. As the aeroplane descended upon the Australian terrain, my heart was a mélange of emotions – apprehension, excitement, and an overwhelming sense of achievement. Tears of gratitude marked my arrival; they were tears for the dreams pursued against all odds, for the courage to trust my instincts when they whispered of distant possibilities. I knew my mum would be so proud, she always said she wanted me and the boys to live there, I had talked of my dreams since I was a little girl, so she knew how much it meant to me. During conversations with her, she used to say she would love the boys to have an Ozzie accent.

My arrival in Australia symbolised more than a geographical change; it represented a profound shift within me. It affirmed my long-held belief that sometimes, the heart's quietest whispers are the loudest calls to action. Trusting my gut instinct, especially when the dreams it harboured seemed so distant and daunting, was not just a choice but a necessity. This journey from the familiar streets of my childhood to the foreign yet welcoming shores of Australia was a testament to the power of dreams and the resilience of the human spirit. I could have made excuses, I could have said I am a single mother, I don't know anyone in Melbourne, I haven't got enough money, I don't know where to start etc. But I didn't, there was no way I was letting my kids down, I had to practice what I had been preaching to them.

In these global ventures, from country to country, I discovered facets of myself previously unknown. Each place I lived in or visited added a unique brushstroke to the canvas of my life, enriching my experiences and broadening my worldview. These journeys were not merely about physical travel; they were voyages of personal discovery and growth, each step an integral part of my evolution from a dreamer to a doer, from a seeker to a finder.

I want to express that it is more than just a recount of travels; it's a narrative of transformation. It highlights the importance of stepping out of our comfort zones, embracing the unknown, and the profound impact of diverse cultural experiences on personal growth. It's a story of chasing dreams, turning the wanderlust into a journey of self-discovery and resilience, and ultimately, finding a home not just in a place, but within oneself. I have often said when your heart is born to roam, anywhere is home!

An Australian Dream, Challenges, and Unexpected Turns

The fulfilment of my Australian dream was a momentous event for my boys and me, but it was not without its hurdles. Just days before I was set to embark on this new chapter, an unfortunate fall down the stairs resulted in a broken patella. This incident, however, did not dampen my spirit. I was resolute in my decision to move, firmly believing that true fulfilment often lies beyond our comfort zones. "Off I hopped," literally and metaphorically, ready to start anew and heal in the land down under.

However, this move brought with it a challenge far greater than I had anticipated. A few months into my Australian adventure, I faced a significant medical setback – I had been misdiagnosed it transpired I had femoral nerve palsy not just a broken patella. This left me disabled for years, plunging me into a new realm of physical and emotional struggles. It was a relentless test of my resilience, a chapter in my life marked by battles on multiple fronts.

During this trying period, medical professionals commended my psychological strength. I drew my strength from a profound appreciation for life, recognising how much worse my fall could have been. "I could have hit my head, or broken my back," I often reflected, grateful yet frustrated by my situation. The physical limitations imposed by my condition brought fear and anguish, feelings of disempowerment that seeped into various aspects of my life, including my relationship with my children, forming a relationship with someone else, the limitations it caused in my work life etc.

The adventurous activities I once shared with my children – tree climbing, swimming with the dolphins, go-karting – were now beyond my reach. I found myself side-lined, a spectator to their enjoyment rather than an active participant. Yet, even in these moments of limitation, we found joy and laughter. Our trips to the zoo, for instance, became memorable not just for the animals we saw but for the roles we humorously reversed – my children pushing me around in a wheelchair, our laughter echoing through the pathways. We don't pity our family, we do humour, and we will always happily tease and laugh at each other.

This chapter of my life taught me an invaluable lesson: even amid great achievements and joys, setbacks are an inevitable part of our journey. It's not the setbacks themselves but how we respond to them that shapes the quality of our lives. My experience showed me that resilience isn't just about bouncing back from adversity; it's also about finding laughter and joy during struggles, about transforming challenges into opportunities for growth and deeper connections. About learning from experiences to help others.

I didn't find transition as an expat hard, Australia is where I felt I was always meant to be, even if things weren't quite the way they were described in the interview, I never once regretted this. There is no such thing as a midlife crisis only a midlife opportunity. There are sometimes complexities when it comes to achieving dreams and we all can face unexpected challenges. This part of my story is that it underscores the importance of resilience, the power of a positive outlook, and the ability to find joy in life's simplest moments, it is a testament to the belief that while life may throw us curveballs, our response to these challenges can lead to profound personal growth and enriched experiences.

The Journey to becoming a Coach and Therapist: A Pathway of True Discovery and a Return to Self

My period of recovery, after my femoral nerve operation meant I had a pause from work, this blossomed into a pivotal phase of mental rejuvenation and introspection. It was during this time, fuelled by a quest for motivation and continuous self-improvement, that I found myself drawn towards the world of coaching – a field I had long considered with keen interest. The deeper I delved into the realm of coaching, the more it resonated with me, I recall, reflecting on how this newfound passion gradually took root. The idea of becoming a coach had been a lingering thought since 2013 when I looked at a network marketing opportunity, it was the mindset aspects that intrigued me and led me through this transition. Everything we go through leads us to exactly where we are meant to be.

Embarking on this journey involved confronting and overcoming my doubts and fears. Achieving my coaching certification was not just an academic milestone but a transformative journey that propelled me into a new chapter of life. I learned to navigate the intricate landscape of self-promotion and self-belief.

The experience of being a coach has been nothing short of extraordinary. It provided me with a platform to assist remarkable women in building their businesses and brands, helping people with their emotional and physical pain, while simultaneously fuelling my own personal and professional growth.

I've always harboured a burning desire to lead an extraordinary life, I declare, acknowledging my innate drive for a life that transcends the ordinary. This journey of coaching and self-discovery has been a thrilling adventure, one where I rediscovered myself, shattered my limiting beliefs, and wholeheartedly embraced an abundance mindset. This is why I set up the coaching mastery academy to help others learn how to release their limiting beliefs, gain their coaching certificate and give them everything they need to set up their coaching practice.

Despite always maintaining a positive outlook, I had never experienced such an extended period away from work with time to reflect," I ponder, recognising the transformational impact this introspective period had on me. It was an unexpected gift of time, allowing me to reconnect with my inner self, re-evaluate my priorities, and redefine my path.

In supporting others to achieve their dreams and goals, I discovered a profound sense of fulfilment. This journey underscored an essential realisation: success is not preordained or limited by one's past or circumstances. This epiphany opened doors to a life of financial independence, personal satisfaction, and the opportunity to contribute meaningfully to causes that deeply resonate with me.

In this book chapter, I have shared the transformative journey of becoming a coach and therapist and how it led to a profound rediscovery of self. It's a narrative about overcoming internal fear and barriers, finding purpose in empowering others, and the realisation that success is boundless. This part of my story is a testament to the power of personal growth and the impact it can have not just on one's own life, but on the lives of others as well. This section of the book not only serves as a window into my past but also as a testament to the transformative power of adversity. It is a reminder that our beginnings do not dictate our endings and that within each challenge lies the potential for growth and rebirth.

> *"Be unapologetically you and allow your dreams to come true!"* - Amanda Brenkley

Amanda Brenkley
Author, Coach, Therapist and Trainer
Founder and CEO of the Coaching Mastery Academy
As seen on Fox TV and Cosmopolitan and Authority magazine

Website: www.amandabrenkley.com
Apply to work with me
Website: www.amandabrenkley.com/experience
Linktree: www.linktr.ee/amandabrenkley37

Scan the QR code below to connect with me

PART 1

Fear Unleashed: Conquering Fear and Anxiety to Ignite Success

"Fear is a reaction. Courage is a decision." – Winston S. Churchill

Fear and anxiety can be a pervasive force that can manifest in various forms, and this is a common challenge that I, as a therapist and coach, often assist individuals in navigating. It's a familiar companion for all of us, making appearances during pivotal moments such as interviews, dates, public speaking engagements, or exam sessions. During these instances, feeling anxious is a perfectly normal response.

However, for some, anxiety becomes an unrelenting presence that refuses to subside, exerting a continuous impact on their daily lives. While I've helped many individuals grapple with such persistent anxieties, today, my focus is on the anxiety and fear that interposes itself between you and your business success and creating a life you god damn deserve!

At its core, anxiety often originates from a worry—a triggered thought that begs introspection. When you sense this unease, take a moment to explore its source. Avoid labelling it as "your anxiety," as ownership fosters attachment. To break free from anxiety and self-sabotage, refrain from claiming it as your own. The root of anxiety lies in the feeling of insecurity, and it prompts me to ask: Were you fortunate enough to have positive role models during your formative years? Did you have individuals in your life who demonstrated how to regulate heightened emotions and navigate feelings of unsafety?

In the realm of business, anxiety can manifest in various ways—procrastination, self-doubt, self-sabotage, overwhelm, reluctance to start, constant distractions, time pressure, negative self-talk, analysis paralysis, imposter syndrome, and perfectionism, to name a few. While these might seem innocuous, it is perfectionism, for instance, that can paralyse us, hindering us from taking the crucial steps needed for business growth. You might find yourself tirelessly working but avoiding the very activities that would propel your business forward and yield tangible results. It's crucial to recognise that these feelings, beliefs, and behaviours offer a false sense of certainty—a deceptive shield of safety. However, you can convince yourself that you are stronger than the grip of anxiety and fear.

Yet, the question persists: Why do we succumb to these patterns? The answer lies in the conflict between conscious desires and unconscious inclinations, manifesting in behaviours that often sabotage our progress. Exploring the concept of the subconscious mind offers profound insights into human behaviour, especially when examining the frequent discord between our conscious desires and unconscious inclinations. This dichotomy plays a pivotal role in shaping our actions and reactions, often in ways we don't immediately understand.

Understanding the Subconscious Mind:

The subconscious mind operates below the level of conscious awareness, influencing our actions and decisions without our active realisation. It's a repository of our past experiences, beliefs, and memories. It functions continuously, even when we are not consciously thinking, and influences our behaviour based on ingrained patterns and past experiences.

There can be conflict between the conscious and unconscious. Our conscious mind is where rational thinking, planning, and decision-making occur. It's aligned with our current goals and aspirations. However, the subconscious mind can hold deep-seated beliefs and fears that may not align with our conscious intentions. These can include limiting beliefs formed in childhood or through negative experiences.

This conflict manifests in self-sabotaging behaviours when our unconscious fears or beliefs overpower our conscious goals. For instance, a person may consciously desire success but subconsciously fear it due to past experiences of failure or a deep-seated belief of unworthiness. These subconscious beliefs can trigger behaviours that directly conflict with our conscious goals, like procrastination, avoidance, or self-doubt.

Self-awareness is key to recognising these patterns. Techniques such as mindfulness, journaling, and reflective practices can help bring subconscious thoughts to the surface. Understanding the origin of these beliefs is crucial. Therapy or self-help methods can be used to unearth and understand these deep-seated subconscious beliefs. The goal is to align the subconscious mind with conscious intentions. This can be achieved through practices like affirmations, visualisation, and cognitive-behavioural techniques. Consistent reinforcement of positive beliefs and goals helps rewire the subconscious, gradually reducing the impact of negative patterns on our behaviour.

When aligned, the subconscious mind can be a powerful ally in achieving our goals. It can enhance creativity, intuition, and motivation, driving us towards our aspirations more effectively. The journey to understanding and aligning the subconscious mind is deeply personal and transformative, leading not only to the achievement of specific goals but also to overall personal growth and emotional well-being. In essence, the power of the subconscious mind is a double-edged sword. Left unchecked, it can undermine our efforts, but when understood and aligned with our conscious mind, it becomes a formidable force in the pursuit of personal and professional success.

Herein lies the dilemma: many individuals remain unaware that they are unwittingly obstructing their own paths, hindering them from attaining their deepest desires in both life and business.

In the chapters ahead, I will share fundamental concepts that not only transformed my own life, and the lives of my clients but also the lives of the amazing women who are featured in this book. I intend to guide you toward a breakthrough, enabling you to discover your passion and purpose.

John Dewey once said...

> *"We don't learn from experiences; we learn from reflecting on experiences."*

When auditing your feelings, try to be open with yourself and don't let your mind hijack you. Be honest because most of us are honest people, but sometimes we are not so honest with ourselves. Have you ever wondered why we engage in self-sabotaging behaviours that hinder our progress? What compels us to stand in the way of our own success? Here, I will shed light on the intricate workings of the mind, highlighting three key functions:

Protect:

Our mind, in its wisdom, is designed to protect us. It acts as a vigilant guardian, shielding us from potential harm or discomfort. This protection often manifests as an inclination to stay within our comfort zones—a familiar space that guards us against disappointment and shields us from the perceived perils of failure. While this mechanism is rooted in the intention of preserving our well-being, it inadvertently limits our growth and potential.

Punish:

Amanda succinctly captures the paradox of "no pain, no gain." Some individuals subconsciously embrace suffering or expect it, viewing it as a form of self-punishment. This self-imposed hardship may stem from a belief in what one deserves or a subconscious acceptance of struggle as an inherent part of the journey. Unravelling this pattern requires a shift in perception and recognising that growth need not be synonymous with suffering.

Prioritise Self (Attention):

The pursuit of attention can also be a driving force behind self-sabotage. In seeking recognition and acknowledgement, individuals may unconsciously adopt behaviours that draw attention to themselves. This attention-seeking mechanism is a strategy to fulfil unmet needs, providing a sense of validation and acknowledgement. Understanding this dynamic allows for a more conscious redirection of these energies towards positive, growth-oriented endeavours.

As we delve into the intricate landscape of our minds, acknowledging these mechanisms becomes a crucial step in dismantling self-sabotage. By unravelling the protective layers, re-evaluating our relationship with pain, and redirecting attention-seeking tendencies, we pave the way for transformative growth and the realisation of our fullest potential.

Embark on a journey of self-discovery and clarity:

Current Self-Assessment

Health: How do you currently rate your physical health? Are there aspects you're proud of or areas you wish to improve?

Financial Status: Reflect on your current financial situation. Are you where you hoped to be?

Relationships: Evaluate the state of your personal and professional relationships. Are they fulfilling and supportive?

Business/Career: Consider your career or business achievements. Are they aligned with your aspirations?

Spiritual Fulfilment: Assess your spiritual or philosophical beliefs and growth. Are you on the path you desire?

Emotional Well-being: How is your mental and emotional health? Are you generally content, stressed, or seeking change?

Other Personal Areas: Think about any other areas that are important to you. How satisfied are you with your progress in these areas?

One-Year Projection

Health: Envision your health a year from now. What changes or achievements do you see?

Financial Goals: Picture your financial status in a year. What milestones are you aiming to achieve?

Relationship Dynamics: Imagine the evolution of your relationships. What improvements or changes do you foresee?

Business/Career Progression: Visualise your career or business a year ahead. What accomplishments do you anticipate?

Spiritual Journey: Reflect on your spiritual or philosophical path. Where do you see yourself in a year?

Emotional Health: Project your emotional well-being a year into the future. What state do you aspire to be in?

Other Personal Priorities: Think about other significant areas. What are your goals and expectations for these in a year's time?

Overcoming Barriers: Identify any fears or worries that might be hindering your progress towards these goals. What are they?

Reflect honestly: Did you restrain yourself when envisioning your future? Why might that be?

Notice if your aspirations shift when you think about them. Do you gravitate towards one goal but then change your focus?

Vision vs. Reality

Imagine a scenario where no obstacle exists and where your potential is limitless. In this ideal state, are your visions aligned with your current aspirations? Or does it transform? This contemplation can illuminate the true extent of your ambitions and the challenges you may need to address to realise them.

If you suspect that self-sabotaging behaviours are hindering your progress, it's important to recognise that these can manifest in myriad ways, varying significantly from person to person. However, certain patterns often emerge.

Common signs include:

1. Resorting to avoidance tactics, such as procrastination, delaying tasks, or failing to initiate actions.
2. Experiencing a deep-seated aversion and discomfort towards change.
3. Feeling persistent negative emotions, marked by an underlying sense of struggle and resistance.
4. Harbouring a fear of personal failure and a belief in your own inadequacy.
5. Believing that opportunities and successes available to others are somehow out of your reach.
6. Fearing judgment from others, constantly worrying about their perceptions and opinions.
7. Experiencing chronic worry, fear, anxiety, or stress.
8. Engaging in harsh self-criticism, often accompanied by a negative and punitive inner dialogue.
9. Adopting a pessimistic outlook, viewing situations and outcomes through a lens of negativity.
10. Imposing unrealistic standards of perfection on yourself, where anything less is deemed unacceptable.
11. Battling feelings of insufficiency, constantly feeling as though you are not enough.

These behaviours and thought patterns are not just obstacles; they are signals pointing towards underlying issues that need addressing for personal growth and development. To effectively address and manage fear or anxiety, it is crucial to first pinpoint its origins. Frequently, the root of anxiety lies not in external factors but within us. The notion that anxiety or stress exists independently "out there" is a misconception. In reality, our internal state significantly influences our external experiences and perceptions. By understanding and auditing these inner sources of anxiety, we can better control how they impact our interactions with the world around us.

Mindset Blocks: Breaking Free from Self-Created Obstacles

Many individuals speak of encountering roadblocks on their journey, often attributing them to external factors. However, the truth is, more often than not, we are the architects of our most formidable barriers through our own thought patterns. It's imperative not to allow external opinions to diminish your worth, and equally crucial is to deny yourself permission to do so.

Our mental landscape is a fertile ground for the cultivation of these self-imposed blocks. Phrases like "I can't do this," or "I lack the necessary degrees," "I'm not articulate," or "I'm a single parent with limited time, skills, and resources" are but a few examples of the barriers we construct. Such thoughts may further manifest as beliefs like "I lack the support from others" or "I wasn't born into a successful family." The refrain of "No one likes me, so I won't be able to get people to buy from me" echoes through the corridors of self-doubt. Recognise these for what they truly are—excuses. Excuses are the architects of limiting beliefs, and the question you must confront is: What excuses are you telling yourself? To create the life you desire and deserve, you must shed these limiting beliefs. We either find excuses or we find reasons.

You don't have to wait for a crisis to spur you into action. While you may have heard stories of breakthroughs emerging from challenging circumstances, you have the power to decide and act now. The question that echoes through the pages of your journey is: Are you ready? Ready to shatter the self-imposed constraints, rewrite your narrative, and embrace the transformative changes that will lead you to the life you envision and truly deserve. The power to decide rests in your hands; the time for change is now.

What stands between you and your desired life? Many individuals point fingers at their parents, others, their educational experiences, or the lack of wealth, among a myriad of possibilities, as the culprits for not living the life they envision. The challenge, however, lies in a perpetual fixation on the past—a haunting landscape that casts shadows on both the present and future. The echo of "if only" reverberates through their thoughts: "If only I were born into money," or "If only I had been luckier back then." The crux is that "if only" never paves the way to achieving a goal.

The danger emerges when we become ensnared in a cycle of dwelling on the past or imagining a negative future, losing sight of the present moment. Instead of focusing on what we are doing and creating a plan for the future, we inadvertently surrender to the grip of regret and self-doubt. The key lies in maintaining a mental presence in the here and now, trusting that everything is unfolding as it is meant to be. Observe your mind and body attentively during this process, for therein lies the transformative power to break free from the shackles of the past.

Furthermore, we tend to project problems into the future that have not yet occurred and may not even materialise. These ingrained beliefs and thought patterns impede optimal performance in both business and life.

Consider this: every negative feeling emanates from a negative thought. The following diagram provides examples to illustrate this crucial connection. Recognising and dismantling these negative thought patterns is the gateway to unleashing your potential and paving the way to a more fulfilling and successful life.

Thoughts	Emotion/Feeling	Action/Result	Outcome
What if I fail, what if I am not good enough, what if I go blank on a live or make a mistake, what if no one buys from me, what if I lose everything.	Anxiety, fear, panic, nervousness and/or overwhelm.	Stress Procrastination Self-Sabotage Analysis paralysis Denial Low Confidence	In action. give up, failure, under achievement or struggle. Which reaffirm the emotion and feelings.
You might tell yourself you will never improve, get started or become successful.	Hopelessness, dissatisfied, self-disgust. discouragement or un-motivated, Uninterested.		
I will never be able to do, it is not available to me, I am not worth it, not good enough, I don't even know where to start.		Low Self-Esteem Affect your ability to think or act rationally. Defensiveness (both a feeling and a behaviour) Undefined goals	And this is how you can get stuck in negative thinking loops.
You tell yourself you not as good as others, you compare yourself. You're not as good, because you aren't as clever, rich, qualified or I don't have what they have.	Inadequate, incapable Imposter Syndrome, lack of self-belief, feeling incompetent, burn out and/or pessimistic	Physical Illness Distraction Perfectionism Resistance	
Self-condemnation, you tell yourself and believe you have failed to live up to your blueprint, this isn't the way it should have been.	Shame or guilt, worthlessness.	Being consumed by failure	
You feel the world treats you unfairly, it isn't your fault, you can't set up or sustain a business, it's everyone else's fault. The network marketing company, the coach you use.	Frustrated, angry, annoyed, irritated, or bored.		

PART 2

Mindshift Mastery: Reflecting on the Power of a Flourishing Mindset

"The mind is everything. What you think you become." – Buddha

In this section, we delve into the intriguing question: What distinguishes a successful individual from others? This quest leads us to examine the profound influence of mindset on our lives. We often witness similar situations yielding vastly different outcomes for different people. But why? The key lies in understanding how each person perceives, interprets, and responds to events, mainly driven by their mindset.

A flourishing mindset is not just about positive thinking; it's a complex interplay of beliefs, attitudes, and perceptions that shape our reality. We explore the concept of 'mind shift mastery,' a process of cultivating a mindset that consistently fosters growth, resilience, and success. This involves:

Through real-life examples, scientific research, and practical exercises, this book aims to guide you in recognising and harnessing the power of a flourishing mindset. You will learn how shifting your mindset can transform your approach to challenges, enhance your ability to achieve goals, and ultimately lead to a more successful and fulfilling life.

Example:

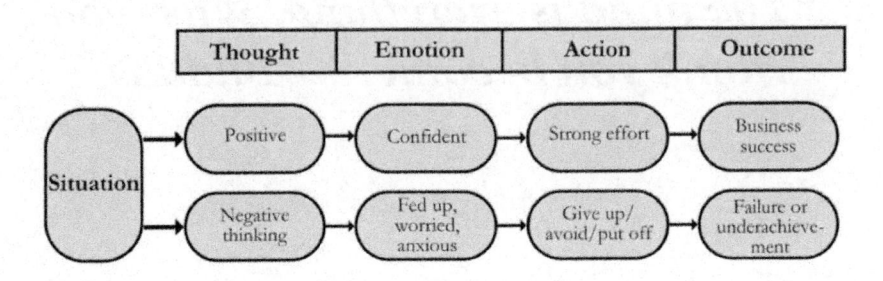

	Thought	Emotion	Action	Outcome
Situation	Positive	Confident	Strong effort	Business success
	Negative thinking	Fed up, worried, anxious	Give up/ avoid/put off	Failure or underachievement

To effectively chart your path to success, consider adopting a reverse engineering approach. Begin by vividly envisioning your desired outcome, and then methodically deconstruct the process to determine the necessary thoughts, feelings, and actions that will lead you there. At this juncture, precise knowledge of how to achieve your goal isn't essential. Instead, concentrate on identifying and nurturing the mindset that will facilitate a favourable outcome. Allow yourself the liberty to daydream, creating detailed mental images of your ideal business and life scenarios.

Contemplate what you aim to achieve through this exercise. Is it a reduction in worry, an increase in resilience, or a surge in self-confidence? Recognise that along this journey, feelings of frustration, anxiety, and stress might surface. While such emotions are natural and sometimes inevitable, it's crucial to ensure they don't overpower logical thinking. Emotions often trump logic when we're not consciously aware of our mental processes. However, by bringing these feelings into conscious awareness, you can start to initiate meaningful change.

Reverse engineering your route to success empowers you to clearly define and understand the steps necessary for achieving your intentions. It's about fostering the right mental and emotional environment to enable the journey towards your aspirations, rather than getting bogged down by the minutiae of the process. This approach not only clarifies your path forward but also aligns your inner resources – thoughts, emotions, and actions – towards achieving the success you envision.

In the wake of these aspirations, it's natural to encounter feelings of fear, frustration, anxiety, and stress. While these emotions are part of the human experience, it is imperative to prevent them from overpowering reason. Emotions tend to triumph over logic when left unchecked, but conscious awareness of this dynamic is the first step toward change. Bringing these emotional responses into the spotlight empowers you to instigate meaningful transformations.

What thoughts do you need to reframe to achieve a better outcome?

Identifying incongruences in your journey is pivotal to achieving the desired outcome. When there's a misalignment between your aspirations and fears, it's crucial to unearth the secondary gains—those subtle advantages derived from not attaining your goals. For instance, the fear of failure might offer the illusion of safety within your comfort zone. Every action, even our worries and fears, serves a purpose, though this purpose may elude conscious awareness.

It's common to burden ourselves with anticipatory stress, fretting over scenarios that may never materialise. Research suggests a staggering 85%-91.4% of our worries remain unrealised. Acknowledging your struggle is the initial stride toward triumph. Silent suffering is not a prerequisite for growth. Sharing your concerns with trusted individuals—be it friends, family, or a colleague—opens doors to external perspectives, possibly unveiling insights and solutions otherwise overlooked. This principle extends to business, where vulnerability and security must find equilibrium. Seeking support alleviates anxiety, providing solace to a troubled mind.

Entrepreneurial anxiety can be paralysing, yet taking the first steps need not involve fixing your gaze on the entire mountain. Expressing your thoughts, whether through conversation, journaling, meditation, or other means, releases the grip of avoidance and alleviates anxiety. Effective problem-solving requires discerning the root cause—be it stress, anxiety, fear, or procrastination—and addressing it comprehensively to prevent recurring symptoms.

Amid the thriving trend of entrepreneurial communities, mental health issues often lurk in the shadows. Recognising your responsibility to yourself and your staff is paramount. As you navigate the multifaceted dimensions of your feelings, understanding and addressing the root causes will pave the way for a more resilient business and a healthier entrepreneurial journey.

Delving into the realm of mindset and self-reflection is pivotal, and while we won't plunge too deeply into the intricate landscape of business coaching as I do with my clients, there are invaluable tools in this book that can fortify your entrepreneurship.

At the heart of these tools is self-reflection—an indispensable aspect of your core operations. Transparency, especially with yourself, is the linchpin. Pausing to reflect, without succumbing to analysis paralysis, allows you to identify areas of misalignment.

Beware of the pitfalls of imposter syndrome or comparison syndrome, as both can be potential breeding grounds for procrastination.

Fear is an omnipresent companion in life, but when allowed to steer your business ship, it can thwart progress or magnify the struggle. A healthy dose of fear can be constructive, but an excess may lead to procrastination or outright avoidance. Similarly, anxiety, often irrational, can act as a dream stealer. Consciously acknowledging and managing these emotions empowers you to regain control.

The importance of looping every decision back to your WHY cannot be overstated. Remaining focused on your overarching vision while surrendering to it allows you to weather day-to-day challenges without losing sight of your ultimate goal. Regularly revisiting your WHY serves as a wellspring of mental and emotional energy, propelling you forward until objectives are met.

Fostering a growth opportunities mindset transforms challenges into avenues for growth, realignment, and success. Instead of questioning why a door is closed, ask yourself what lessons can be gleaned and what opportunities may arise from the situation.

Discovering and transforming limiting beliefs about money is a pivotal aspect of your journey towards financial empowerment; this is why I teach money mindset in my SMASH program. As often, these beliefs are deeply rooted in our childhood experiences and narratives. To reshape your financial story, it's essential to challenge and reframe these ingrained mindsets. The transition from restrictive thoughts, such as "money doesn't grow on trees," to empowering affirmations, like "I attract money with flow and ease." This shift in perspective can profoundly influence your financial trajectory, fostering a more positive and abundant mindset towards wealth and prosperity. By consciously choosing to adopt affirmations that resonate with abundance and possibility, you open the door to a more prosperous and financially fulfilling life.

Drawing from personal experience, I've come to understand the profound impact of re-evaluating past beliefs and narratives. For instance, consider the frustration often associated with dyslexia. Such a narrative can either act as a barrier or be a source of empowerment. By shifting the perspective and recognising dyslexia not as a hindrance but as a unique gift, one can unlock a wellspring of creativity and distinctive strengths. The real challenge lies in pinpointing and letting go of those limiting beliefs that act as anchors, holding you back from realising your full potential. It's about transforming perceived weaknesses into sources of strength and innovation. This process of introspection and reframing not only alters your self-perception but also opens up new avenues for personal growth and success.

The exercise presented invites you to sit in the feelings of accomplishment to envision the goal, intention, or outcome. By visualising, feeling, and hearing the success, you bring it to life, reinforcing the positive mindset required to overcome obstacles and propel yourself towards success. In the end, understanding and reshaping your beliefs, coupled with intentional self-reflection, forms the bedrock for a resilient and thriving entrepreneurial journey.

Crafting a more empowering narrative is the cornerstone of transforming your life story. It all begins with understanding that the beliefs you hold are the architects of your limitations, and the key to unlocking your potential lies in the art of reframing your thinking.

Seizing control is not just an option; it's a necessity. Recognise the inherent power within you—the power to initiate change, reshape your beliefs, and craft a narrative that galvanises you forward. When you tell yourself, "I can't help the way I feel," you inadvertently cast yourself as a victim of circumstance. While external factors undeniably exert influence, their impact is not as pervasive as commonly perceived. You are the master of your mood, the curator of your dreams, the architect of your aspirations.

It's crucial to clarify that advocating for perpetual happiness is not the objective. Embracing a full spectrum of emotions is part of the human experience. There will be moments of negativity and sorrow, but the true essence lies in not relinquishing control to these emotions. Acknowledge that you have the power to navigate through a range of emotional states without being enslaved by them. This realisation is a powerful tool in expediting your journey out of challenging emotional states.

The empowerment here lies in understanding that you are not a passive recipient of your feelings but an active participant in their orchestration. By exercising this awareness, you reclaim agency over your emotional landscape. This newfound sense of control doesn't negate the validity of negative emotions; rather, it empowers you to navigate through them with resilience, emerging on the other side stronger and more in command of your narrative.

In essence, the shift towards a more positive and constructive narrative starts with recognising your ability to steer the ship of your emotions and beliefs. By doing so, you not only transcend the limitations imposed by external factors but also embark on a journey of self-discovery, resilience, and personal growth. This narrative, one of empowerment and conscious control, is the tapestry upon which a better and more fulfilling story of your life unfolds.

PART 3

Boundaries of Brilliance: Goal setting for Fearless Triumph

"Set your goals high, and don't stop till you get there." – Bo Jackson

Embarking on the entrepreneurial journey ushers in a profound shift, particularly in the realm of autonomy. The allure of freedom that drew many to entrepreneurship can paradoxically become challenging as a discipline is thrust into the spotlight. For a venture to thrive, structure and foundation are imperative, yet the pursuit of autonomy often clashes with the need for a well-defined structure. It's a delicate balance that every successful business must navigate.

The Autonomy Paradox

The pursuit of autonomy, a driving force for many entrepreneurs, requires a dance with discipline. It's a paradoxical challenge that demands attention from the outset. As the entrepreneurial path unfolds, the need for a well-defined structure becomes evident. Without a solid foundation, ventures are susceptible to chaos. This chapter delves into the complexities of maintaining autonomy while establishing the necessary boundaries for success.

Mastering the art of saying 'no' is an essential skill in the quest for a balanced and fulfilling life. It requires the discernment to evaluate opportunities not merely based on their allure or potential benefits but through the more nuanced lens of your personal values, beliefs, and guiding principles. This process involves a conscious alignment of your choices with what truly matters to you.

For instance, if family is a central pillar in your life, it becomes imperative to establish clear boundaries that honour this value. This might mean making a firm commitment to avoid work-related activities or travel on Sundays, reserving this time exclusively for family. Such a decision not only demonstrates your commitment to your loved ones but also ensures that your professional life does not encroach upon precious family time. In addition to setting aside specific days, consider the implementation of 'techno days' - designated periods where digital devices are set aside. These device-free intervals are dedicated to fostering deeper, more meaningful connections with family members, free from the distractions of emails, calls, or social media. By creating a space devoid of technological interruptions, you ensure your presence with your loved ones is complete and undivided.

Incorporating these practices into your routine isn't just about saying 'no' to external demands; it's about saying 'yes' to what you value most. It's a deliberate choice to prioritise and nurture the relationships that bring joy and meaning to your life. Through these actions, you create a harmonious balance between your personal and professional worlds, allowing you to live more authentically according to your core values.

Navigating the entrepreneurial path inevitably brings its own set of hurdles, not least among them the presence of energy-draining influences - often referred to as the 'vampires' of the business world. These can be the perennial pessimists, the 'Debbie Downers', or those who consistently radiate negativity. One critical step in combating this toxicity is exerting control over your digital environment.

In the age of social media, where interactions are frequent and far-reaching, it's vital to be vigilant about the kind of energy you allow into your space. This may mean taking decisive actions such as muting, unfollowing, or even blocking sources of negativity on these platforms. Such measures are not just about avoiding unpleasantness; they are a proactive strategy to protect and preserve your mental energy.

By curating your digital surroundings, you create a more positive and inspiring online environment. This, in turn, supports the maintenance of a positive mindset, which is crucial for entrepreneurial success. It's about consciously choosing to surround yourself with content and connections that uplift, motivate, and align with your goals and values. In doing so, you not only enhance your personal well-being but also fortify the mental resilience needed to navigate the complexities of the entrepreneurial journey.

Goal setting is a common source of frustration for many entrepreneurs. The gap between setting goals and actualising them can lead to feelings of failure or doubt. Understanding the intricacies of the mind is pivotal in overcoming these hurdles. Taking action involves embracing the **SMART** goals framework:

-**S**pecific and Simple: Clearly straightforwardly define your goals.

-**M**easurable and Meaningful: Make your goals quantifiable and personally significant.

-**A**chievable: Ensure your goals are within reach.

-**R**ealistic and Responsible: Ground your goals in reality and hold yourself accountable.

-**T**ime and Toward Set a timeframe and direction for your goals.

Reflection and Forward Momentum

The goal-setting process extends beyond the annual ritual. Reflection on the past is integral to shaping the future. Before crafting goals for the upcoming year, this chapter advocates delving into the experiences and lessons of the current year, both personally and professionally. This reflective process sheds light on growth and evolution, highlighting shifts that have occurred. The importance of letting go is emphasised, as it opens up space for new opportunities and growth.

In the midst of this reflective process, the act of writing down goals becomes a transformative exercise. Take the time to contemplate your aspirations, articulate them on paper, and witness the power of reflection and clarification. This intentional practice not only solidifies your vision but also propels you forward with purpose and determination on your entrepreneurial odyssey.

In the world of entrepreneurship, the adage holds true: "You can't hit a target you can't see." This chapter concludes with the importance of maintaining a clear vision through intentional goal-setting, boundaries, and reflection. By mastering the delicate balance between autonomy and structure, entrepreneurs can navigate the complexities of their journey with fearless triumph. The boundaries of brilliance are set, providing a roadmap for success in the dynamic landscape of entrepreneurship.

PART 4

Self-Care Symphony: Nurturing the Entrepreneurial Soul

"Caring for yourself is not self-indulgence, it is self-preservation, and that is an act of political warfare." – Audre Lorde

Navigating the tumultuous waters of life, particularly during challenging times, is a universal experience that many individuals face. The current landscape, characterised by elevated stress levels and pervasive uncertainty, has amplified the struggles individuals encounter in their day-to-day lives. The delicate juggling act between personal life and professional pursuits often tilts the scales, plunging individuals into the depths of overwhelm, anxiety, and self-doubt. If you find yourself resonating with these sentiments, rest assured that you are not alone.

In this intricate tapestry of existence, where stress and uncertainty seem to loom at every turn, regaining control and fostering a sense of well-being becomes paramount. This chapter explores comprehensive stress-busting strategies, delving into practical tips and holistic approaches that empower individuals to not only weather the storms of life but also to thrive amidst the challenges.

Understanding the Landscape of Stress:

Before delving into the strategies for stress management, it's crucial to understand the multifaceted nature of stress. In today's fast-paced and interconnected world, the demands of daily life can easily become overwhelming. Balancing the responsibilities of personal life and the pursuit of entrepreneurial endeavours adds a layer of complexity. The desire for autonomy, often a driving force behind entrepreneurial aspirations, can paradoxically lead to a lack of structure, exacerbating the feelings of overwhelm.

The initial step towards effective stress management involves recognising that stress is a natural response to life's challenges. However, allowing stress to dominate one's life and perpetuate a cycle of anxiety requires intervention. This chapter aims to provide a guide to help individuals take charge of their mental and emotional well-being.

Stress Busting Tip 1 - Regaining Control:

The first tip in the stress-busting arsenal is centred around regaining a sense of control. When overwhelmed, it's common to feel as though circumstances are spiralling out of control. However, the reality is that there are more elements within an individual's control than they might realise. The challenge lies in shifting focus from what seems uncontrollable to discerning what can be managed.

A practical exercise recommended by stress management experts involves a visual representation. By drawing two circles on a piece of paper—one inside the other—a person can create a tangible visualisation of what is within their control and what lies beyond it. In the inner circle, individuals can list factors they can control, ranging from daily routines to personal reactions to situations. In the outer circle, factors that are beyond immediate control are identified. This visual aid serves as a powerful tool in bringing awareness to the areas where action can be taken.

The next step is to identify one specific action that can be taken to address a controllable aspect and work from there. This process is not about miraculously solving all problems but rather about taking incremental steps toward regaining a sense of control. Equally important is the practice of releasing the concerns that fall outside the realm of control. This acknowledgement and intentional release set the stage for a more empowered mindset.

Stress Busting Tip 2 - Clearing the Mental Space:

Stress often becomes a cumulative burden when concerns from the past infiltrate the present. Clearing mental space involves letting go of yesterday's worries and anxieties, as well as refraining from excessive concern about the future. This approach is rooted in the understanding that one cannot live in the past nor control every aspect of the future. The present moment, therefore, becomes the focal point for well-being.

A common phrase echoes the sentiment, "Don't carry things with you from the past, as you don't live there anymore." This principle is equally applicable to future **concerns**.

It is counterproductive to put off happiness with thoughts like, "I'll be happy when I am rich" or "I'll be happy when I quit my job." Happiness is a choice to be made in the present, irrespective of external circumstances.

Mindfulness practices play a pivotal role in unloading mental burdens. This involves actively choosing to be present in the moment and letting go of past regrets and future anxieties. Strategies include sharing concerns with a trusted friend, creating a list of areas where support is needed and assigning them to different individuals, switching off from negative news, and engaging in positive self-talk.

Being kind to oneself is another crucial aspect of clearing mental space. Internal narratives often tend to be harsher than the dialogue one might have with others. The journey toward well-being starts with self-compassion. Be Kind, when directed inwardly, serves as a reminder to treat oneself with the same kindness and understanding offered to others.

If these recommendations sound simplistic, it's because they are intentionally straightforward. The power lies in their simplicity. Resolving to release worries from yesterday and focusing solely on the now initiates a profound shift in mindset. As individuals breathe out negativity and consciously release the grip of stress, they set the stage for elevating their vibration and energy levels.

Beyond the external strategies for stress management, the chapter emphasises the significance of internal practices such as mindfulness and finding one's inner quiet place. In a world filled with incessant noise and demands, carving out moments for inner stillness becomes a valuable asset.

The exercise involves going deep inside to a place where a sense of peace prevails. It's about consciously creating a mental sanctuary where tranquillity reigns. By taking deep breaths and immersing oneself in this inner quiet place, individuals can experience a profound sense of calm. This internal retreat serves as a refuge where worries, regrets, disappointments, and anger can be acknowledged and gradually dissolved.

Acknowledging negative emotions as non-serving is a pivotal step in this process. Having faith in one's ability to act with total confidence, embracing happiness, and fostering self-assurance are crucial components of this internal journey. Scientifically validated, meditation emerges as a potent tool for relaxation, offering a myriad of benefits, including stress reduction, anxiety control, enhanced self-awareness, and improved sleep.

Stress Busting Tip 3 - Visualisation and Gratitude:

The third stress-busting tip revolves around the practices of visualisation and gratitude. Visualisation entails picturing specific acts aligned with personal preferences—perhaps a leisurely walk, gardening, or engaging in yoga. This simple act, combined with a quiet and calm mind, creates a mental sanctuary where individuals can retreat. These moments of quiet and calm, when practised daily, unlock the potential for heightened productivity and a sense of accomplishment.

Coupled with visualisation, gratitude becomes a powerful force against stress. The act of consciously recognising and appreciating positive aspects of life carries transformative power. The recommendation is to write down things one is grateful for using a journal, paper, or even an envelope. The act of physically penning down these expressions of gratitude intensifies their impact.

Reflecting on the positive occurrences in one's life before bedtime becomes a daily ritual. Questions such as "What made you feel good today?" or "What made you laugh?" prompt a journey into the day's positive experiences. This reflective practice also includes acknowledging moments of joy, instances of assistance provided to others, and personal achievements that evoke a sense of pride. By cultivating a habit of focusing on the positive, individuals naturally elevate their energy levels and create a buffer against stress.

Stress Busting Tip 4 - Healthy Living:

The final tip in the comprehensive stress-busting guide addresses the foundational aspects of healthy living. The symbiotic relationship between physical and mental well-being is undeniable. Stress can easily be exacerbated by neglecting fundamental aspects of self-care, such as proper nutrition, hydration, regular exercise, and adequate rest.

Limiting the intake of stress-inducing elements, such as salt, sugar, caffeine, and alcohol, forms the dietary cornerstone for stress management. Hydration, often overlooked, plays a crucial role in nourishing vital organs and maintaining overall well-being. Adequate water intake rejuvenates the skin, hair, and internal organs, contributing to a holistic sense of health.

Regular exercise emerges as a potent stress-busting strategy. Physical activity releases endorphins, the body's natural mood enhancers, resulting in increased energy levels and emotional well-being. Exercise not only promotes physical health but also acts as a natural antidote to stress, providing an outlet for pent-up tension and anxiety.

Adequate and restful sleep is another cornerstone of stress management. The body and mind require sufficient sleep to rejuvenate and prepare for the challenges of the day. Struggling with sleep is a common stressor, and addressing this concern is pivotal for overall well-being. I offer a free sleep meditation as a resource for those seeking assistance in improving their sleep quality, you can access this at amandabrenkley.com.

Conscious breathing is a simple yet effective technique for stress reduction. Deep belly breaths infuse the body with pure oxygen, promoting relaxation and centring the mind. Laughter, often dubbed as food for the soul, is encouraged as part of a healthy living regimen. Engaging in activities that bring joy and spending time on personal pursuits contribute significantly to stress reduction.

Building and nurturing healthy relationships further fortify the foundation of a balanced life. Engaging in meaningful connections and addressing any issues that may threaten the closeness with loved ones are essential components of stress management. The permission to indulge in activities that bring personal joy and a sense of fulfilment is a crucial aspect of self-care.

This chapter culminates with the recognition that contentment and balance in life act as powerful buffers against everyday stresses. When individuals prioritise self-care and consciously create a balanced life, they become better equipped to face unexpected challenges with resilience and confidence. This holistic approach to stress management acknowledges the interconnectedness of physical and mental well-being, emphasising the importance of a proactive and intentional approach to healthy living.

Invitation to Holistic Business and Well-being Retreats:

For those seeking a deeper immersion into the practices discussed in this chapter, Amanda extends an invitation to well-being retreats. These retreats adopt a holistic approach, focusing on gentle exercise, mindset cultivation, and nutrition. Set in peaceful and beautiful surroundings, these retreats provide individuals with the opportunity to concentrate on their holistic well-being.

To explore more about these retreats or to receive additional support in managing stress. Amanda offers free discovery calls for those who are serious about making change. These calls serve as a platform for individuals to connect, discuss their unique challenges, and explore personalised strategies for living a life empowered, in control, and confident. Interested individuals can reach out to amanda@amandabrenkley.com for further details.

In conclusion, the journey to effective stress management involves a multifaceted approach that encompasses self-awareness, intentional actions, mindfulness practices, and a commitment to healthy living. By incorporating these comprehensive stress-busting strategies into daily life, individuals can foster a resilient mindset, elevate their well-being, and navigate the complexities of life with confidence and grace.

PART 5

Strategic Brilliance: Mastering the Art of Fearless Execution

"Strategy is about making choices, trade-offs; it's about deliberately choosing to be different." – Michael Porter

Embarking on the entrepreneurial journey is akin to navigating uncharted waters. In this dynamic landscape, success is not merely a destination; it is a continuous journey marked by strategic planning, mindful delegation, celebratory milestones, stress management, and a profound understanding of oneself and the business environment. This chapter aims to unravel the intricacies of a comprehensive entrepreneurial strategy, providing a roadmap for success.

Strategic Planning: The Foundation of Success

The transition from a productive day to a strategically planned tomorrow is a ritual that separates thriving entrepreneurs from the rest. As the day concludes, a 10-minute brain dump becomes a pivotal exercise. Prioritising tasks from the most crucial to the least ensures that the next day begins with a clear roadmap. This proactive approach not only enhances productivity but also frees the mind from the burden of unresolved tasks.

In tandem with the brain dump, maintaining a journal emerges as a therapeutic practice. Entrepreneurs externalise their thoughts onto paper, addressing lingering concerns and stressors. The act of structured planning offers mental clarity, allowing entrepreneurs to face the next day's challenges with a focused mindset.

The Power of Delegation: Easing the Burden

Entrepreneurship often comes bundled with overwhelming responsibilities. The early stages of a start-up demand a discerning evaluation of tasks—identifying what only the entrepreneur can do and what can be delegated. The willingness to delegate becomes inversely proportional to anxiety levels. Relinquishing control over tasks that can be handled by others frees entrepreneurs from the shackles of overwhelming stress.

Delegation is not a sign of weakness but a strategic move to optimise resources. Discerning tasks that align with one's unique skills and competencies is key. Trusting and empowering a team fosters a collaborative environment where each member contributes their strengths for the collective success of the business.

Celebrating Wins: Nurturing a Positive Culture

In the tumultuous journey of entrepreneurship, celebrating victories, irrespective of their size, becomes a crucial practice. Entrepreneurship can be isolating, especially for those without a business partner or life companion. Acknowledging and celebrating small achievements injects positivity into the entrepreneurial journey. Focusing on what is going right creates a positive energy field, attracting more favourable outcomes.

Celebrating wins is not limited to external achievements; it's also about honouring personal growth and resilience. Entrepreneurial success is a cumulative effect of numerous small victories. By cultivating a habit of celebrating daily wins, entrepreneurs cultivate a mindset of gratitude and optimism, which is essential for navigating the challenges that lie ahead.

Slow Down and Set Priority Stages: Mastering Entrepreneurial Stress

The rapid pace of entrepreneurship often propels individuals into a perpetual state of stress. Recognising that the entrepreneurial journey is a process, not perfection, is crucial. Perfection is an elusive ideal, and setting unrealistic expectations only amplifies stress. Prioritisation emerges as a strategic imperative. Identifying what is truly important and time-blocking the day accordingly helps avoid constant reactivity.

Time-blocking, a simple yet effective strategy, segments the day into manageable slots, ensuring that essential tasks are attended to without succumbing to anxiety. Balancing the urgency of tasks with a forward-looking approach allows entrepreneurs to proactively address stress points and minimise reactive firefighting.

Breaking down monumental tasks into smaller, achievable steps is another tactic to navigate the complexities of entrepreneurship. This incremental approach not only facilitates progress but also provides multiple opportunities for celebrating victories along the way. Every step, regardless of size, contributes to the overarching goal, making seemingly insurmountable challenges more manageable.

SWOT UP: Leveraging Strengths and Opportunities

A strategic entrepreneur is well-versed in the SWOT analysis—knowing the Strengths, Weaknesses, Opportunities, and Threats. Amidst the rigours of challenging tasks, it is easy to lose sight of the progress made. Recognising individual strengths, as well as those of the team, is a leadership skill that drives effective delegation and fosters a holistic business approach.

Understanding the strengths and weaknesses, not only of oneself but also of the team, allows for the optimal utilisation of resources. A business thrives when its people are in good health, physically and mentally. Prioritising self-care becomes imperative for an entrepreneur, as personal well-being directly influences business health.

The quote by Thomas A. Edison serves as a poignant reminder that success often lurks just beyond the point of perceived failure. The strategic entrepreneur remains attuned to their journey, leveraging strengths, mitigating weaknesses, and seizing opportunities while navigating threats.

Conclusion: The Harmonious Symphony of Strategy

In conclusion, the entrepreneurial journey is a symphony where strategic planning, delegation, celebration, stress management, and self-awareness harmoniously converge. Entrepreneurs equipped with a well-thought-out strategy navigate the unpredictable terrain of business with resilience and foresight.

This chapter serves as a guide, emphasising the transformative power of strategic thinking in shaping a successful entrepreneurial journey. It is not merely about reaching a destination but about the continuous evolution and refinement of strategies to thrive in an ever-changing landscape. As entrepreneurs implement and adapt these strategies, they not only steer their ventures towards success but also cultivate a mindset capable of overcoming any challenge that arises in their entrepreneurial journey.

> *"Many of life's failures are people who did not realise how close they were to success when they gave up". Thomas A. Edison*

PART 6

Halt the Hesitation: Breaking Free from the Chains of Doubt

"Doubt kills more dreams than failure ever will." – Suzy Kassem

In the dynamic landscape of personal and professional growth, one of the pivotal junctures revolves around overcoming hesitation and self-doubt. This chapter serves as a guide, offering actionable strategies to break free from the chains of doubt and welcome transformative change. The journey to unleashing your potential involves navigating through self-reflection, reframing negative thoughts, taking responsibility, and envisioning a future steeped in success.

Pause and Reflect: Shifting Perspective

The initial step in this transformative journey is to pause and reflect. It's a moment to cease self-blame for every perceived mistake and acknowledge that each misstep is a lesson on the path to business growth and personal learning. The realisation that no one is perfect and that we are all in a perpetual state of learning is fundamental, as we are all just humans living a human experience.

Embracing imperfection is not a flaw but an opportunity for growth. Understanding and internalising this concept is crucial to changing the narrative. As you navigate the challenges of entrepreneurship, consider each setback as a stepping stone, a valuable lesson that contributes to your evolution.

Reframe Negative Thoughts: Harnessing Positivity

Negativity can be a formidable adversary, and mastering the art of reframing is a powerful tool in your arsenal. Create a mental sanctuary filled with positivity, whether it's through motivational songs, empowering phrases, or personal mantras. These elements serve as anchors, grounding you when faced with challenges.

When negative thoughts emerge, consciously reframe them into constructive and optimistic perspectives. Identify a power phrase or a go-to motivational anthem that resonates with you. These tools can alter your state of mind, instilling confidence and resilience. It's a conscious effort to reshape your internal dialogue and cultivate a positive mindset.

Take Responsibility without Blame: Enjoying the Journey

Taking responsibility is a cornerstone of personal and professional growth, but it should not be misconstrued as self-flagellation. The key is to embrace accountability with grace, acknowledging mistakes without descending into blame. The entrepreneurial journey is a dynamic mix of highs and lows, challenges, and victories.

Rather than blaming external factors or others, the focus should shift to enjoying the journey. Embrace each moment, play with it, and find joy in the process. If limiting beliefs persist and hinder progress, seeking support through coaching or hypnotherapy can be a transformative step. The goal is to navigate challenges with resilience and a sense of adventure.

Level Up: The Game from Heart and Soul

Transformation need not be a protracted process; it can happen in an instant. Observing clients undergo profound changes in mere seconds is a testament to the power of focused interventions. This transformative journey is likened to a game—one that originates from the heart and soul.

As you embark on this journey, envision your success story. Define what success looks like for you, envisioning the unique capabilities and triumphs you desire in the future. The emphasis is on the heart and soul of the transformation, where the change is not only tangible but resonates on a profound level.

Craft Your Success Story: Envisioning the Future

Crafting your success story involves creating a compelling narrative of the future you envision. Consider the unique capabilities you wish to possess and the triumphs you aspire to achieve. What is the better story you want to tell a year from now? By visualising your achievements, emotions, and the sounds associated with your future triumphs, you set the stage for their realisation.

This exercise is not merely about setting goals but creating a vivid mental image of your success. It's about aligning your aspirations with a narrative that resonates with your deepest desires. The process involves defining your unique capabilities and triumphs, giving shape to the story you want to tell.

Morning Routine Top Tips: Setting the Tone

How you start your day often determines its trajectory. A mindful morning routine can be a powerful tool in setting a positive tone. The key tips include avoiding immediate phone usage, reflecting on yesterday's victories, practising gratitude, acknowledging today's wins, engaging in physical movement, and setting intentions for the future.

Consider the desired work-life balance, the number of weeks off work, ideal working hours, and activities to exclude from your upcoming year. Re-evaluate past decisions that may no longer align with your evolving self. Identify the person you need to become to achieve these intentions. This exercise is about shaping your path consciously and aligning your actions with your envisioned future.

Vision Exercise: Manifesting Your Desires

The vision exercise involves transporting yourself to the end of your envisioned success. Close your eyes and engage your senses—feel it, hear it, see it. This immersive exercise serves as a powerful catalyst for translating your vision into actionable steps. With a clear mental image, take the necessary actions to transform your aspirations into reality. This exercise is a culmination of the envisioning process, translating the mental image of success into tangible steps. By engaging your senses, you create a vivid and compelling vision that serves as a guiding light on your journey. In the words of C. Bard, *"Though no one can go back and make a brand-new start, anyone can start from now and make a brand-new ending."* The journey toward overcoming doubt and embracing transformation begins with a conscious choice to rewrite your narrative.

It is a journey marked by intentional reframing, accountability, joy in the process, and a relentless pursuit of your envisioned success. As you embark on this transformative book experience and now move into reading about the influential women in this book and their powerful stories, remember that the power to shape your ending lies within you.

This exploration into unleashing your potential is not just pages or chapters in a book; it's an invitation to embark on a transformative journey that transcends the pages. It's a roadmap to self-discovery, resilience, and the creation of a narrative that resonates with your deepest aspirations. As you turn the pages of this book, let it serve as a catalyst for the brand-new ending you are about to create.

Next Steps

Embark on a transformative journey with me, and together we will implement change and make a significant impact in your life. I offer three distinct pathways to cater to your unique needs and aspirations:

Personal Healing and Growth:

If your goal is self-healing and personal development, I provide a one-on-one service that encompasses hypnotherapy. This also includes coaching and full access to my **SMASH** program, a transformational experience with a proven framework designed to elevate women with:

Strategies for Getting Over Anxiety

Money Mindset

Anxiety around Relationships

Strategies for Business Success

Harnessing Confidence

Upgrading you both emotionally and financially. This program is ideal if you're ready to take a significant step forward in your personal journey or entrepreneurship.

Becoming an Inspirational Coach:

For those eager to support others, I invite you to join my Coaching Mastery Academy. This comprehensive program employs a triangulated approach: you'll not only learn everything needed to become an inspirational coach, but you'll also participate in the SMASH program for your own development, receive a coaching certification, and gain essential business skills to establish or enhance your coaching practice. We also provide a full done-for-you service, where we can set up your business with you, taking the68tresss and overwhelm away whilst you concentrate on the elements that you are passionate about.

Business Development through a VIP Retreat Experience:

If you're looking to establish or elevate your business, consider our exclusive 4-day subversives VIP retreat in Murcia Spain. This intensive experience involves working closely with me and my team to delve deep into your business 121, providing strategies for success. We'll assist you in various aspects, including copywriting, social media, website development, funnels, content creation, photography etc. all aimed at elevating your business and generating leads. This is a tailor-made service to support your business needs but also allows for time for well-being and relaxation.

For those interested in other forms of collaboration, there are additional opportunities to work with me at various investment levels. Discover more about these options and embark on your path to transformation, by visiting my website amandabrenkley.com. Let's start this journey together and unlock your full potential.

Apply to work with me
Linktree: www.linktr.ee/amandabrenkley37

> *The real contest is always between what you have done and what you are capable of doing. You measure yourself against yourself and nobody else.'... Geoffrey Gaberino*

CHAPTER 2

Loretta Jeffery

Life Coach, specialising in Anxiety, Stress, Low Self Esteem and Overwhelm

Launchpad Beginnings: Decoding Where to Start and Why?

My name is Loretta Jeffery, I live in the West Midlands with my husband and 2 children, and I have suffered with anxiety, low self-esteem, not feeling enough, imposter syndrome, a general feeling of lack, plus more, throughout my life. Having experience and knowledge in this area, by using the methods I use, one of my life goals is to help others get through these struggles and come out the other side, a happier, healthier and resilient person.

When I was given the opportunity to write a chapter in a book, my inner voice immediately said 'no way you can't do this, no one will be interested in your story' but my intuition told me otherwise.

I feel I have so much to share with those who are or have struggled with anxiety, shyness, low self-esteem, overwhelm, and not-enoughness, I could go on more. To be in this place is soul-destroying, tiring, frustrating, with a 'lack of' mentality and can affect your life in a big way. Who wants to feel like this and live their life in this way? Not me!

Our daughter has ASD and ADHD, and our son has ASD, both of them particularly struggle with anxiety. I have suffered from anxiety from the age of 7 and was diagnosed with GAD – Generalised Anxiety Disorder in 2012. For years I read about phobias, why we have them, where they can come from and how to overcome them. I went to a Hypnotist in 2008 where 'regression' was used, and I found out where my phobia had come from. When I was 7 years old, I was involved in a car accident with my family. Fortunately, my dad, brother and myself, apart from a few scratches and bruises, were ok, but my mom wasn't, she had severe head injuries. We had to sit on the side of the road, waiting for the ambulance, while my mom kept being sick and was obviously not well at all. With thanks to the Doctors and Nurses, my mom was ok.

On our journey home from the hospital, my mom found it stressful and kept being sick. So, my vomit phobia made complete sense. However, despite knowing where the phobia had come from, this didn't help with my anxiety, every time someone would even mention the words sick, vomit or not well, made my anxiety spiral out of control, my throat went dry, my heartbeat raised, I couldn't sleep, I felt clammy all over and was on high alert, it was exhausting! When I had my children, my phobia got worse, I was constantly worrying that they would pick up a sickness or stomach bug from school and parties. Holidays abroad always made me feel anxious as I was constantly worrying that someone would either get food poisoning or sunstroke, I couldn't relax, parties were the same, and I found myself not going to a lot of them, fearing that people would drink too much alcohol and be sick. It was endless and built up to a social phobia too. I was beginning to feel anxious about anything and everything.

I was referred for CBT – Cognitive Behaviour Therapy, I had 6 sessions, which helped a little, but I felt I needed more. My therapist suggested I look at taking medication, so after speaking to my Doctor, I reluctantly started taking medication for depression and anxiety. I am still on this medication and one of my life goals is to completely stop taking them and be able to control my anxiety without them.

Unyielding Resilience: How to Persevere and Never Give Up

When I was at school, I was always the shy, quiet girl, so I let myself believe that this was a bad trait to have, that I would be like it forever and it couldn't be changed. I had, and still do, have a happy family life and feel blessed. Both my dad and brother have the same heart condition Atrial Fibrillation (AF), my dad suffered a heart attack whilst on holiday in Spain, fortunately, the hospital team were great and my dad was able to come home after 2 weeks. At the beginning of COVID my dad was lucky and was able to have a heart bypass, which fingers crossed, has done its job and my dad can now live a normal life, my daughter keeps him on his toes and he is often in floods of (laughter) tears, which warms my heart and I feel very lucky and proud that they have this relationship.

My brother had to spend a Christmas day in hospital, fortunately, he has a wonderful, loving and caring wife who is always by his side, they are each other's rocks. Amongst all of this, my Mom has survived 2 encounters of breast cancer.

Our son was born with a large hole in his heart, this wasn't picked up until his 6-week check-up. This was a very hard time of our lives, he was too tired to take or drink much milk, and he wouldn't take to a bottle, so I was his only form of food, he wasn't thriving and slowly deteriorating. At 11 weeks old he underwent open heart surgery, the staff at Birmingham Children's Hospital were beyond fantastic, they looked after all of us, and talked us through each and every step. After 1 week our son was able to come home, we felt it was a miracle.

However, he still wouldn't take to a bottle and due to the stress, I was struggling to produce enough milk. A friend suggested seeing a Cranial Osteopath, knowing we had nothing to lose, we tried it, and it worked! At 8 months old, our son took to a bottle and began to thrive, getting stronger and stronger each day. He now leads a completely normal life, he still has check-ups and hasn't yet been fully discharged, but fingers crossed, he will not need any more surgery. We feel like the luckiest parents in the world.

Our daughter and son have Autism and ADHD, so life can be very challenging, particularly when out of their routines, like holidays, birthdays and Christmas. They both suffer with anxiety, but in different ways. Our daughter has a tick that becomes worse during anxious times – she will grimace, be very hyperactive, zone out and be angry, she won't talk about it. Our son will school refuse, get very angry, suffers with sleep problems, and will zone out, but will try to talk about it. As an anxiety sufferer myself, I am able to understand and empathise with them and use my patience (although at times this can be difficult!). Their mental health is always forefront of my mind.

At the time of writing this, I am a part-time PA, my aim was to go back to work full-time when my children got to secondary school, but due to struggles with their neurodiversity and mental health, I am fortunate to be able to remain working part-time. I have worked with my employer for over 17 years, so we have a good working relationship which works well on both sides. I have a good work ethic and always have since I started working.

MasterCraft: My Ultimate Toolkit for Success

The reason I share my story is because I was able to get through these life events. All through my life I am constantly learning and working on my personal development and have built an ongoing toolkit.

Mindset is a big part of everything. A mindset is a person's established set of attitudes, beliefs, and assumptions that shape their perception and approach to various aspects of life. It influences how individuals interpret situations, make decisions, and respond to challenges or opportunities. Mindsets can be fixed or growth-oriented, impacting one's ability to adapt, learn, and navigate the world.

A healthy mindset can have numerous benefits. It promotes resilience, allowing you to navigate challenges with a positive outlook. It enhances overall well-being by reducing stress and fostering emotional stability. A healthy mindset also supports better decision-making, as it encourages a balanced perspective and adaptability. Additionally, it can positively impact relationships, as it often involves qualities like empathy, understanding, and effective communication. Overall, a healthy mindset contributes to a more fulfilling and satisfying life.

Amongst many others, manifestation / The Law of Attraction is one of the items in my toolkit. Manifestation often involves setting clear intentions, visualising your goals, and taking tangible steps toward them. I try my best to stay positive, believe in my abilities, and align my actions with my aspirations to help manifest my desires. The Law of Attraction is a belief that suggests positive or negative thoughts bring positive or negative experiences into a person's life. It's based on the idea that focusing on what you want can attract those things. I like to use visualisation and affirmations to align my thoughts with my desires. Many years ago, I visualised being married, with 2 children – a girl and a boy, have a dog and live in a village. I now live in the village that I manifested, I am married, with a daughter and son, and a shihtzu. It was only when I started learning more about manifesting that I realised that it does actually work!

I also try not to get too overwhelmed, when I feel myself going down this path, I break down tasks into smaller steps, prioritise what needs my immediate attention, and consider reaching out for support. I take a moment to breathe or engage in activities that bring comfort e.g. journalling, yoga, essential oils, or meeting a friend for a coffee.

I find journalling can be therapeutic, it provides a space for me to express thoughts and emotions. It helps me to self-reflect, clarify goals, and reduce stress. Regular journaling enhances self-awareness and can contribute to personal growth.

Self-care is crucial for overall well-being. It involves practices that prioritise my mental, emotional, and physical health. This includes activities like making sure I have adequate sleep (which isn't difficult because I love to sleep!), regular exercise, reading, yoga, my essential oils, making time for my friends and family and eating healthily. Taking time for self-care helps recharge my energy and contributes to a more balanced and fulfilling life. If I am not looking after myself, then I am of no use to everyone around me.

I always try to be as resilient as I can, this is a work in progress and I am working hard on being able to bounce back from adversity, adapt to challenges, and endure difficulties, this is through cultivating resilience through coping strategies, a positive mindset, and learning from setbacks.

Every few months I think about what is holding me back, e.g. fear, lack of confidence, low self-esteem, people pleasing, worrying about what others think, and I write it down on a piece of paper, I then burn or tear it into little pieces and feel the negative energy leave me.

InspireSphere: Navigating the Source of My Creativity

I feel lucky and fortunate enough to have met a lot of 'Teachers' along my journey of personal development. The first was being gifted 'The Power Is Within You' by Louise Hay, I refer back to this book regularly. It gave me an introduction to how to begin transforming my life by changing my thoughts and beliefs, the connection between thoughts, emotions, and physical well-being, and encouraging positive affirmations and self-love as tools for personal growth and healing.

At the beginning of COVID, I began to look further into self-esteem and realised how low my self-esteem was. I joined a programme based on self-esteem and put a lot of the tools into action, it is a gradual process which involves delving deeper into self-awareness, the use of positive affirmations – by replacing negative thoughts with positive affirmations, setting realistic goals, being kind to yourself and by learning and growing.

I have the pleasure of working with a Life Coach, Essential Oil Mentor and Yoga teacher, all of these together are my passions! I have attended various courses with her, such as 'You Are Enough', 'Comparisonitis', 'Gratitude', 'Imposter Syndrome', 'Flow with Ease' and 'Overwhelm'. I have a wonderful collection of essential oils that I use to lift me, and my family, psychologically, particularly when we are feeling anxious, stressed, ill and when we are struggling to sleep, to lift our moods and I use them in my daily skincare. They are toxic-free too. I don't leave the house without my peppermint oil! I use my oils when attending any of Karen's courses. I attend a yoga class every Thursday evening and try to include the practice during my self-care time. I love how Yoga emphasises the connection between the body and mind, through physical postures, breath control, and meditation, cultivating awareness, and promoting a sense of balance and calmness. After a stressful day, I look forward to yoga as it is also a relaxation response, by activating the parasympathetic nervous system. This counteracts the "fight or flight" response, leading to a state of relaxation and reduced stress. We use various different breathing techniques, my favourite is the Ujjayi Breath, which involves breathing in and out through the nose while slightly constricting the back of the throat. This produces a soft, ocean-like sound, enhancing focus and concentration.

At the time of writing this, I am studying and training to be an NLP Practitioner, the course Leader is one of the World's leading life coaches and NLP'ers. NLP is used to enhance your ability to behave positively and constructively. I am captivated by his knowledge, wisdom and enthusiasm. I use the techniques and incorporate them into my life as and when I feel they are needed.

I also work with a Goal Setting Coach. This is a powerful process that helps me to plan and achieve what I want in various aspects of my life. Alongside this I do my 'weekly wins', I initially found this difficult but realised I was overthinking it, so started to write down even my little wins, such as my son going to school without getting upset, crossing something off my to-do list etc. On days when I feel I haven't achieved very much, I write down my daily wins and immediately feel better about it.

I am part of a wonderful group where I have learnt so much about building a business, but also about mindset and how the two go hand in hand, it's like my business bible!

Last, but definitely not least, I feel very lucky to have met and work with Amanda Brenkley, Therapist and Coach. As soon as I heard one of her trainings, I felt drawn to her, I love her passion kindness and understanding, and how genuine and relatable she is. I learn something new in every discussion, training and lesson, and I can put all my learnings over the years together.

Forward Horizons: Paving the Way for Journey Ahead

One of my life goals has been to get to the bottom of overcoming anxiety and to help both my children. This then leads on to helping others to stop feeling the way I did with my anxiety and everything that goes with it, as let's face it, it sucks!

Amongst others, I use the above strategies daily. On waking up, I do a 5-minute meditation (as this is always achievable, anything longer is always a bonus). I look at my day ahead in my planner. I have my own affirmations that I look at, a different one each day, and often with an essential oil. I walk my dog, getting out in the fresh air, even when it's wet and cold, always lifts my mood. I do my best with being present, everything I do I make sure is achievable and realistic, so anything I do on top is always a bonus. I eat as healthy as I can (I have a sweet tooth so some days can be harder than others), I keep on top of my water intake and listen to my body when I haven't had enough, which shows in the form of a headache, feeling tired, not having full concentration and sometimes irritability. I have flavoured teas (often ice teas in the warmer weather) if I get bored of water. I will write anything down that comes into my head, that I can't deal with at the time, I carry post-it notes around with me! At bedtime I will either write down or say in my head, my gratitude for the day, on the days that I think I don't have any, I will always think of something, even if it's being grateful for having my 2 beautiful children, for having a roof over my head, especially when the weather isn't good.

As mentioned above, at this time of writing this, I am studying and training to be an NLP Practitioner (Neuro-Linguistic Programming). One of my favourite aspects is 'Anchoring'. This uses the concept of anchoring, where specific stimuli become associated with a particular emotional state. By anchoring positive states, you can recall and experience those states in challenging situations. I use this when my anxiety heightens around sickness, I also use it with my children when they feel anxious, particularly around going to school.

Using all the tools above, to also include mindfulness, resilience, wellness plus more, I have built a coaching practice. Everything I learn, I want to pass on to others and help with their journey through life. I am constantly learning and adding more to my toolkit. Not every situation has the same strategy, so I find it helpful to mix them around, according to the situation.

Life should be enjoyed, filled with passion and purpose, but sometimes obstacles are put in our way, at times we don't see it, but they are often put there to help us to learn and grow, and we come out of it a better person.

Inner Essence with Loretta

If you would like access to my free Guide to Mental Fitness, or for further information on how to book a call with me, please visit my website below. Facebook: https://www.facebook.com/loretta.1612

Website: www.inneressencewithloretta.com

> *"What you think, you become. What you feel, you attract. What you imagine, you create."*

CHAPTER 3

Terri Brown

PR Strategist

The early days

I was teaching when I first realised that there had to be more to life than this endless cycle of work, sleep, and work that I seemed to be trapped in. Spreading myself across three different departments in a local college, two for 16 to 18-year-olds studying vocational courses and one for mature students doing an access course, was a real challenge but one I relished. My time in the classroom was fantastic. I loved watching the students learn, putting the theory into practice on their placements and then reporting back and telling me how it went.

However, there is a lot more to teaching than simply being in the classroom. The expectations were so high that in order to complete all the required tasks, I was working twice as many hours as I was being paid for, as well as studying for an additional qualification at the same time. I had two young children at home, and despite only officially working four days a week, I felt like I was never spending any time with them.

In the evenings, I would return home from work and spend hours in my office marking assignments, writing references for UCAS applications, compiling parents' evening reports, planning lessons and a whole host of other activities that were expected of me, but that time was never officially allocated.

My days were fuelled by stress and guilt. When I was at work, I would spend my time thinking about everything that needed to be done at home. I would worry about which sports day, nativity, or celebration assembly I would miss that week. I would receive pictures from our childminder that were meant to reassure me that our youngest son was healthy and happy, but all they did was act as a reminder of all the things that I wasn't getting to do with him and all the firsts I was missing out on.

Yet when I was at home, instead of enjoying the time with my boys that I craved so much at work, I'd find myself clockwatching, working out how early I could put them to bed so that I could return to my office to continue work, just to ensure that I was in bed before midnight, ready to start again the next day. Weekends were the same. It became a given that the boys would have a Daddy day on a Sunday, and I would stay home and work, catching up on things from the previous week and trying to prepare for the week ahead in a bid to keep on top of things. Neither home nor work, my children, nor my students were getting the best version of me. I had no work-life balance and no social life, and I felt completely lost.

"Sometimes, in order to find your true self, you need to get a little lost."

The tipping point

The tipping point came four years into my time at the college when I was refused leave to attend a family funeral because cover couldn't be found for my classes. It was around this time that I also discovered that whilst I was being required to do an additional teaching qualification in my own time, other teachers were being allowed to not only attend the course in work time but were also being given time to complete the assignments in work time too. It all felt so wrong. I was spinning too many plates, and I simply couldn't continue in this way. My mental health was suffering. I was anxious and stressed and living on next to no sleep, riddled with guilt—something needed to change.

Making the leap

Luckily for me, I had a very supportive husband. He could see that my health was deteriorating and that I simply wasn't happy anymore, so he encouraged me to hand in my notice and leave my role as a teacher despite the fact this would mean a big reduction in our household income.

Even with his support, it wasn't an easy decision to make. Yes, I was struggling, and no, I wasn't happy, but I WAS proud of being a teacher, and I DID love the students. I was also terrified of telling people I couldn't handle it and everyone thinking I had failed, but after some time off where I had space to reflect, I knew I couldn't return, so I left teaching with no plan and no job to go to.

I had a good support network around me. My mum and my husband encouraged me to take some time before I jumped into anything, and due to the fact we no longer had any childcare bills, our household income wasn't affected as much as we feared it would be. While I was figuring out what to do next, I spent time building up my blog, which I had been working on since before I started teaching. It was a little passion project, a form of escapism and something fun just for me. It started to bring in some money and lots of opportunities to attend press trips and review products. It was the perfect balance of life and work, especially as most of the events were ones I could take the kids to, too.

After about a year, I got itchy feet. I felt like my old self again and ready to take on more work. The blog was doing well, but I needed something more. I missed teaching, or at least I missed the actual classroom side of teaching and the interaction with the students, not everything else that came with it. And although I was willing to return to some form of work, I knew I still wanted to maintain the work-life balance I had restored in my life. My youngest was now in preschool, and the eldest was in primary school, so I felt returning to work a couple of days a week would be enough. After some searching, I took on a freelance position, working for a charity, travelling around schools, and delivering history lessons. It was the perfect mix of classroom-based teaching that I missed without any of the additional work or stress.

Everything was going well, so much so we even decided to extend our family, having found the perfect solution that offered a good income but still on my own terms in a freelance position that meant I could take shifts when and if I wanted and turn them down when needed, I would never need to miss a nativity (or funeral) again. I went on maternity leave happy in the knowledge that once our daughter was old enough, I could return to my blog and my freelance teaching role and once again have the best of both worlds.

An unexpected turn of events

But then the unimaginable happened. We were hit by a pandemic. I was home on maternity leave, working on the blog part-time, looking after a baby, and homeschooling two children, one of whom was also studying for the 11 plus. It was crazy. My husband was working in a frontline role, and so after the first few weeks of lockdown, he soon returned to his place of work, leaving me juggling this new routine on my own. As COVID started to ease and schools reopened, my maternity leave finished, but the impact of COVID on education meant that there would be very little work available via the charity for at least 12 months, with what work was available going to those on contracts and not to the freelancers and so, in essence, I had no job to return to and needed to make new plans.

The Strawberry Fountain

Thankfully, I had kept my blog, **The Strawberry Fountain**, going throughout my maternity leave and during the pandemic. It was my saving grace and going from strength to strength, so I decided to give it my all and become a part-time blogger and copywriter. I started writing articles not just for my blog but for other bloggers, as well as for businesses that wanted to run a blog on their website. The work was regular, and it was good. I loved it. I got to work with many different businesses, go on press trips again once the world had reopened and even attend events where my kids were mixing with celebrities. It was fantastic. But I also knew it wasn't making enough money, and if I wanted to keep this work-life balance, then I'd have to rethink quickly as the alternative was returning to full-time employment, something I didn't want to do.

The move to PR

It was then that I realised that there was a massive crossover between what I was doing as a blogger and the work of the Public Relations managers (PRs) with whom I was working so closely.

I spoke to a few of the PRs that I worked with and asked them about their jobs to make sure I wasn't making any significant assumptions or missing anything, and luckily, I wasn't. Their jobs weren't easy, but they were fun, and with my knowledge of the industry and numerous contacts already secured, it felt like a natural progression. I completed a couple of courses in PR, equipped myself with the skills and knowledge that I needed to be successful in this new field, and found myself a mentor. Someone who I trusted and who had done exactly what I wanted to do, go from blogger to Freelance PR manager. I started to put into practice everything I had learned, and it wasn't long before I landed my first client. I'm not going to lie; it was difficult. I found I had no confidence. People would ask me if I had a degree in PR, which I didn't, and that would knock me for six. I'd be terrified they would tell me I wasn't qualified to do the job I was doing. But I ploughed through, learned as I went, and found that I was actually pretty good at it. But there was still the fear of failing. I was so worried about being judged that I wouldn't tell people what I did for a living in order to avoid questions I couldn't answer. It was as if I was embarrassed of my business and the fact that I was no longer a teacher and didn't have a "real job".

I quickly realised there was an issue with my mindset.

Finding my people

In order to make my business succeed, I knew I had to approach it differently. I was terrified of giving this my all in case I failed, but at the same time, I was even more terrified of having to go back to a nine-to-five, a job that would take me away from my children and one where I would have to start asking for permission to go to sports days and beg for time off to look after my children when they were poorly. It was not a life I wanted to return to, so in order to maintain this new life, I needed to believe in myself.

I continued to work with my mentor. I was asking questions, seeking advice, and reading all the books. I needed to feel confident in the PR world so that I could easily tell people what I did and answer their questions. I joined some Facebook groups for people working in PR. I was a long-time lurker in these groups. Reading all the posts and familiarising myself with the terminology. I didn't want to join in with conversations as I was worried I wouldn't fit in. I was scared to ask questions in case they called me out for my lack of experience and asked me to leave, but when I finally joined in and introduced myself, what I actually found was that everyone in these groups was really supportive. I could be totally honest and say that I was new to the industry, and people would offer me their expertise and advice. Everyone was so friendly and supportive, and I'm still in some of these groups today. Only now am I able to offer some of that support and guidance to the new people who join, which is lovely.

But back in those early days, despite this support and my growing confidence, I still felt terrified of putting myself out there, which is ironic when my main objective is to help my clients do exactly that. But I had an actual block when it came to doing it myself. I was getting better at telling strangers what I did. I could talk about PR and share my successful media coverage with ease, but I was still struggling when it came to talking to people I knew, with people who I classed as friends and who I should have been excited to share my news with, but instead, I was avoiding in case the conversation turned towards work which it so often does.

I found I was self-conscious of what I was doing. I felt like I was winging it and suffered massively from imposter syndrome, and I was still worrying that those who had known me as a teacher would still be judging me for failing at that and would be waiting for me to do the same again. I started to share the odd bit about what I was doing on social media, and the reaction was surprising. People congratulated me and asked me for information, and it soon became clear who my cheerleaders were. It also became clear that there were certain friends whose opinions mattered more to me than they should have. I felt they were judging me. They had good, stable careers, and they had openly questioned my blog in the past and asked what I was doing now that I wasn't a teacher. Even though they were no longer close friends or part of my everyday life, their opinions bothered me. I would look for their social media accounts after posting something, hoping they hadn't seen it. Once I realised how much I feared their gossip and acknowledged that this was holding me back, I was able to act on it. I removed them from social media. I made it so they could no longer see my posts, and I unfollowed them so that even if they did post something about me, or something unambiguous that I could convince myself was about me, I would no longer know about it and therefore, it couldn't upset or worry me. This was not an easy task, and it took time to change my mindset from one that needed to be accepted to one that understood I would never please everyone, and that was okay. They weren't my ideal clients, and their opinion, or worse yet, their approval was actually of no consequence to the success of my business.

Once I did this relatively simple task of removing them from my social channels, it was like a big weight had been lifted, and it was a big step towards improving my confidence, self-esteem and most importantly, my self-belief. I could be myself and start promoting my business. I started posting pictures of myself under my business name regularly, and eventually, those fears subsided, and my confidence grew.

I started to use social media more frequently, caring less about what old acquaintances thought and more about what potential clients would think. I also spent more time on social media interacting with people who filled up my cup with joy, whose posts were positive and uplifting and who shouted for others, not at them, celebrating their wins and spreading happiness. It's incredible what a change in your social media intake can make on your own social media presence and overall emotional well-being. And do you know what? It worked. My ideal clients were seeing me, and better yet, they were hiring me.

My PR company has gone from strength to strength. I have had the privilege of helping some incredible entrepreneurs tell their stories and promote their products or services. Watching my clients find the confidence to shout about themselves and share their knowledge with the world as the experts, they never fail to make me smile. I still get excited every time I see my client's interviews or articles in print or listen to them on a podcast or radio show.

Often, my clients come to me with a wonderful business or an incredible product that can help so many people, yet they are too scared to put themselves out there and show the world what they have achieved. I look at them, and I am reminded of myself, and this drives me to not only secure them the media coverage they deserve but also help to build them up on a personal level so that they, too, can believe they are worthy of their success and start to believe that those that matter don't judge and those that judge don't matter.

I've now secured coverage in some of the top magazines, including Stylist, Authority Magazine and Psychologies, and my only regret is that I didn't believe in myself sooner.

If you are starting your own business or have already started but feel unable to progress, my advice to you is to create your own circle of cheerleaders. Join groups of like-minded professionals and get involved in discussions, look at your friends and family, keep your support network close and get rid of the naysayers. Believe in yourself and tell the world what you have to offer.

You can be the best in the business, but they can't hire you if no one knows you exist.

Ready to Take Your Business to New Heights?

Whether you're looking to amplify your brand, secure media coverage, or build the confidence to put yourself out there, I'm here to help. From my own journey—from blogger to successful PR strategist —I've learned the power of self-belief and the importance of having a supportive network.

Let's work together to tell your story, promote your products or services, and elevate your presence in the media. Your success story starts here. Reach out to me today, and let's make those dreams a reality!

Website: www.terribrownpr.com
Instagram: www.instagram.com/terri_brown_pr
Facebook: www.facebook.com/getsocialwithterribrown

CHAPTER 4

Shevanne Helmer

Sacred Feminine Healer and Transformational Life Coach

Whispers of the Womb: A Journey to Sacred Healing
The Awakening

My journey toward embracing the Sacred Feminine and reconnecting with the inner wisdom of the womb has been shaped by a rich tapestry of experiences, both profound and mundane. This path has been underpinned by the persistent queries of Why, How, and What, which have guided me through a lifelong adventure of self-discovery. I took the traditional route quite early in life, stepping into marriage and motherhood in my early twenties. At 21, I found myself married to my college sweetheart, embracing the joys and challenges of raising children. This period in Norway was a time of awakening. Surrounded by strong, supportive women, I began to get glimpses of the Sacred Feminine, though I wouldn't fully grasp its enormity until much later. In Oslo, my days were filled with the energy and rhythm of being a gym instructor and running a dance studio, fostering not only physical strength but a sense of community among women.

It was after leaving Oslo and relocating to the South of France with my two babies, aged four years and six months that I ventured into my creative passions. There, I began designing clothing, merging authentic handmade African fabrics with European textiles. This creative endeavour was a dance of cultures, colours, and textures, a reflection of my journey blending different worlds.

My thirties saw the expansion of my fashion brand and the joy of welcoming my third child. These years were also marked by the reassuring presence of my mother, who visited annually from Miami. Her support gave me the freedom to travel, particularly to African countries, broadening my horizons and deepening my appreciation for my heritage and diverse cultures.

My forties ushered in a period of turbulence and radical change. With my older children being more independent and a divorce, I relocated to Paris from my small village in the south of France. The transition to a single mother in a bustling city, especially with a young child in tow, was a mix of exhilaration and fear. This period, challenging and painful, was marked by internal conflict as I grappled with the ingrained belief that divorce signified failure, a notion my mother often echoed. In hindsight, these tumultuous years laid the groundwork for my deeper spiritual journey.

Born under the sign of Gemini, with a Leo ascendant and a Sagittarius moon, I was graced with a unique blend of energy, adaptability, and a remarkable capacity for multitasking. This astrological combination empowered me not just to handle but truly thrive in juggling multiple life events simultaneously. The curiosity and versatility of Gemini, the warmth and courage of Leo, and the philosophical depth and explorative spirit of Sagittarius all converged to shape my approach to life. These traits instilled in me a profound love for people and an inherent desire to serve, which have been the cornerstones of my journey and contributions for many years.

Entering my fifties marked a conscious shift towards a deeper spiritual path. I explored various healing modalities – from hypnotherapy to psychotherapy, each adding a layer to my understanding of the human psyche. However, it was in the realm of shamanism that I found a profound connection to Earth, the natural world and a sense of belonging that other practices couldn't match.

The enforced solitude imposed by the COVID pandemic became a fertile ground for my spiritual exploration. In the seclusion of my home, I delved into shamanism, Reiki, kundalini yoga, mantras, and tantra and discovered the depths of my inner world. This period of introspection revealed hidden aspects of myself that had been hidden or unacknowledged.

A significant milestone on this journey was my training with Alberto Villoldo and the Four Winds Society, renowned institutions in the world of shaman studies. Villoldo, a prominent figure in modern shamanism, has spent years cultivating a deep connection with the Qero tribe, learning and integrating their ancient practices into the teachings of the Four Winds Society. The Qero tribe, known as the direct descendants of the Incas, are revered for preserving ancient Andean spiritual practices. They specialise in energy healing, rituals, and divination, deeply connected to the natural and spiritual world. My training with the Four Winds Society thus became a bridge to the ancient wisdom of the Qero tribe, allowing me to immerse myself in their profound spiritual teachings.

This path of lifelong learning and discovery has been filled with delight and gratitude. Each step has been a revelation, building my understanding of my role as a healer and guardian of the Sacred Feminine and the Womb. This new period in my life signifies not just a new chapter but a homecoming to my true self and the sacred role I am destined to fulfill.

Embracing the Ancient Wisdom

As an established healer and coach, I sought to deepen my practice and further my personal healing journey. This quest led me to the Four Winds Society's intensive four-week in-person Energy Master training program. The transformative highlight of this journey was the Womb Healing Rite, a profound ritual led by Marcela Lobos, a renowned shamanic teacher, author, and healer. This rite opened a gateway to the wisdom, magic, and healing power inherent in our wombs. It significantly shifted my understanding of healing, refocusing my attention on the trauma within my womb and unveiling a new path to discovering and embracing my Sacred Feminine. This experience not only catalyzed my own deep healing but also inspired me to guide other women on similar journeys, marking a direction in my work I had never anticipated.

Marcela's transformative journey began with a powerful dream in 2014, where she was assisted by four medicine women in birthing a symbolic baby representing ancestral fears and pains. This ceremony, infused with the potent spirit medicine of the jungle and the transformative energy of the Jaguar, served as a profound act of healing for both the participants and Mother Earth. Marcela, entrusted with this Rite, shared it with us, extending its healing power to women worldwide.

On the final day of our program, Marcela bestowed this rite upon our group. It was a life-altering experience that is etched deeply into my being. That night, I was graced with a vivid dream, a symbolic reflection of my life, which unveiled a long-suppressed memory and emotion related to a past abortion. This realisation was both profound and painful, bringing to light emotions and grief I had long buried.

Supported by fellow shamans, we conducted a healing ceremony dedicated to the baby and to healing the wounds in my womb. This ceremony marked a significant turn in my spiritual journey, not just as a healing of my own past trauma but also as an act of releasing and liberating the baby's spirit. This pivotal event spurred my journey toward a deeper embrace of the Sacred Feminine. It served as a stark reminder of the depth of understanding and learning still ahead of me. Eager to continue this path of discovery, I delved into various courses and workshops, exploring tantra and the sacred feminine, each step bringing new insights and deeper connections.

During this period, I found a mentor specialising in Tantra and Healing the Sacred Feminine. Our time together was a journey of both learning and unlearning — a process of shedding old paradigms and embracing new, empowering truths.

This chapter of my life underscored the profound importance of connecting with ancient wisdom. Reconnecting with the past became a bridge to a deeper understanding of healing and the mysteries of the Sacred Feminine. This journey enlightened me about the transformative power of the womb and the collective healing potential of women. As we reconnected with our ancestral roots and wisdom, I began to see the immense healing capacity we hold, not only for ourselves but for our lineage and the broader community. This was the commencement of a broader journey, a path promising to take me deeper into the sacred and mystical realms of the womb.

The Inner Transformation

Welcoming 2023 with a heart full of introspection, I found myself reflecting on a year that had profoundly reshaped my understanding of myself. My journey, a lifelong quest for self-discovery, had led me into the sacred depths of my being, where I encountered hidden paths, each revealing layers of my body's wisdom, the nuanced essence of femininity, and the delicate dance between masculine and feminine energies within me.

This journey, woven with threads of revelation and pain, compelled me to confront long-neglected wounds, particularly those entwined with my womb and the essence of my femininity that I had overlooked. My medical history not only mirrored my mother's struggles but also cast a revealing light on a deeper, more poignant story. Cesarean sections, relentless battles with fibroids leading to severe hemorrhaging, and a series of surgeries – these were not just physical trials. In retrospect, they bore deep emotional and spiritual scars, unmasking the profound impact of these experiences. The initial relief I felt after these surgeries, a liberation from the physical challenges of menstruation and childbirth, soon unfolded into a bittersweet epiphany. This relief, upon introspective examination, laid bare the harsh truth of how I had unconsciously absorbed and lived by societal narratives that estranged me from the sacredness of my own body.

This awakening, this newfound clarity, ignited a desire within me to reconnect with and honour the long-neglected aspects of myself. I had embarked on a journey to understand the legacy of neglect and imbalance that had manifested in my body, a legacy shared with my mother and perhaps generations before her.

Delving into the recesses of my past, I unearthed long-buried memories. I recalled the unspoken but strict expectations placed on me as a child, which were distinctly different from those of my brothers. These societal norms subtly relegated me to the background, a reality starkly contrasting with the freedoms and privileges my brothers enjoyed. This early disparity set the tone for my reluctance to embrace my femininity, influencing my feelings towards everything related to my womanhood, including my relationship with my womb.

Despite this, life had a different plan. It led me down a path of marriage and motherhood, blessing me with three wonderful children who became my guiding light of unconditional love and self-acceptance. They taught me lessons I didn't know I needed, even as I grappled with my own sense of femininity.

Even though my mother had passed away, our journey of healing and forgiveness was rich and profound, spanning years of navigating through shared wounds and traumas. The Rites of the Womb, which I received a year after her passing, added a profound depth to my understanding. This ritual illuminated not only the profound impact of my childhood and life experiences on my feminine energy and womb but also shed light on the heavy burden of misogyny that my mother had carried, a legacy inherited across generations. This awakening transcended personal revelation, showing me how healing oneself can resonate across time, touching the lives of ancestors and influencing future generations. Thus, my journey of healing evolved into an act of reparation and liberation, honoring my mother and extending back seven generations, while also paving a path of empowerment and healing for my daughters and their descendants. Embracing this healing meant mending my relationship with femininity and contributing to breaking the cycle of generational trauma, creating a legacy of empowerment and resilience for women in my lineage.

Acknowledging that my life had been swayed predominantly by masculine energy was a turning point. It led me to seek balance and healing for my womb and to embrace the Sacred Feminine within. This journey was not just about healing; it was about reclaiming and honoring the parts of me that I had unknowingly forsaken.

Dismantling the deep-seated beliefs about femininity has been a journey of enlightenment, unearthing truths that lay buried under societal conventions. Embracing the Sacred Feminine has been a pivotal step in my healing process.

This chapter in my life has been a transformative inward journey, filled with moments of vulnerability, strength, and profound insights, uncovering the resilience and wisdom inherent in embracing my true essence. This process has not just been about self-discovery; it has been a reclamation of the sacredness of my feminine spirit, a celebration of its resilience and beauty.

The Healer Emerges

As I stepped into my 60s, I experienced an epiphany that profoundly reshaped my life's journey. I realized the root of many of my challenges lay in an imbalance of feminine energy, tainted with toxicity, and an overreliance on masculine energy, leading to a disconnect from my essential female nature, especially my womb. This revelation was both startling and enlightening, marking a significant departure from my previous path. This 'aha' moment ignited a fervent quest to understand, heal, and embrace my sacred feminine and my womb. My spiritual guides over the past five years, embodying the sacred feminine, have been Mary Magdalene and Isis. Initially resistant to their teachings and focused on honoring the sacred feminine within, I gradually found myself accepting and integrating this vital message.

As opportunities arose, I became mindful of life's synchronicities, which allowed me to channel and impart higher wisdom. I began hosting evening ceremonies, and rituals focused on healing the sacred feminine and the womb. My commitment to spreading the womb healing rite led me to create workshops and retreats, catering to the growing demand for deeper engagement and understanding.

Working with women on this path has been immensely fulfilling. I've engaged with many seeking to heal various womb-related issues, from PMDD and fertility challenges to menopause and self-worth. The magic of group dynamics in a sisterhood setting has proven profoundly effective for healing the sacred feminine.

One of the most heart warming aspects of this work has been witnessing the transformation in women as they begin to see themselves and each other in a new light. Envision a group of twelve women, initially sitting in a circle, filled with skepticism and uncertainty. As the retreat progresses, their defenses gradually dissolve, allowing them to immerse themselves fully in the healing experience. The transformation is palpable – a shift in energy and a newfound lightness in their expressions.

A powerful testimony to the impact of this work came from a participant who shared her experience: "The retreat was the most wonderful celebration of sisterhood and our femininity. Shevy had created a space for us to open our souls and feel so loved and held by each other. After a difficult breakup and a year of carrying fear and pain in my womb, which had stopped my monthly bleeding, I doubted my femininity. Opening up and feeling supported at the retreat, my bleeding resumed a month later. It was magical, a sign that my womb was at peace with me again, cleansed from fear and pain."

Each ceremony and retreat have been journeys not just for the participants, but also for me. Observing and facilitating these moments of awakening, healing, and transformation has been an indescribably rewarding experience. It has reinforced my belief in the power of embracing and healing the sacred feminine – not just as a concept but as a tangible, life-changing reality. This newest chapter of my life is about stepping into my role as a healer, a guide, helping others to unlock and embrace the sacredness within themselves, and witnessing the beautiful unfoldment of their journeys.

The Continuing Path

As my journey continues, each step on this path of healing and empowerment brings new insights and deeper connections. The evolution from seeking personal healing to becoming a guide for others has been a journey of profound growth and learning. In this chapter of my life, the focus shifts towards the future, contemplating the expansive possibilities that lie ahead in my practice and the wider community of Sacred Feminine and Womb healers.

The process of healing and guiding others has not only been about imparting knowledge or facilitating experiences; it continues to be a reciprocal journey where every interaction, every shared moment of vulnerability, continues to add to my understanding and deepen my connection with the sacred feminine energy. This journey has taught me the importance of continual learning, of being both a student and a teacher in every encounter.

Looking ahead, I envision expanding the reach of my work, aspiring to touch more lives and foster a deeper understanding of the sacred feminine. I dream of creating a space where women from all walks of life can come together to learn, heal, and support each other in a community that cherishes the wisdom of the feminine spirit.

The retreats and ceremonies will continue, each one uniquely designed to address the evolving needs and insights of those who seek healing. I see these gatherings not just as healing sessions but as celebrations of feminine energy, as platforms for sharing stories, experiences, and wisdom.

In the future, I also see myself delving deeper into research and study, collaborating with other healers and experts in the field. This collaboration aims to blend traditional wisdom with contemporary understandings of women's health and spiritual well-being. By integrating these diverse perspectives, I hope to offer a more holistic approach to healing the womb and embracing the sacred feminine.

Another vision that beckons is the creation of a series of written works or online resources. These would serve as guides or companions for those who cannot attend the retreats or wish to continue their journey independently. Through these resources, the wisdom and practices of womb healing can be made accessible to a broader audience, allowing the healing power of the sacred feminine to reach far and wide.

Personal growth remains a constant goal. I intend to deepen my own spiritual practices, continually nurturing my connection with the sacred feminine. This personal growth is essential, as it empowers me to be a better guide and healer. I also see myself mentoring new healers and sharing my journey and learnings to inspire and empower the next generation of sacred feminine and womb healers.

The ultimate aim is to contribute to a global awakening and appreciation of the sacred feminine. It's about creating a world where the feminine energy is honored and celebrated, where healing is accessible to all who seek it, and where the wisdom of the womb is recognized as a vital aspect of our collective well-being.

As I walk this continuing path, I carry the lessons learned, the joys experienced, and the connections made. This path is not just mine but belongs to every woman who has walked it with me and those who will join in the future. Together, we weave a tapestry of healing, empowerment, and transformation that extends beyond our individual lives, contributing to a legacy of honoring and uplifting the sacred feminine for generations to come.

Shevanne Helmer

Sacred Feminine Healer and Transformational Life Coach

Website: www.shevannehelmerlifecoach.com

LinkedIn: www.linkedin.com/in/helmer-shevanne-b17b88 Facebook: www.facebook.com/shevanne

CHAPTER 5

Lucy Foster Paterson

Digital Creator

In the beginning, there was darkness

At 29, I felt a profound sense of disillusionment with my career. Enduring a year-long battle with my employer had left my confidence shattered, casting a shadow over my future. Seeking a fresh start, I explored options at the job centre, but none resonated with me. Frustrated and determined to break free from the past, I chose the path of self-employment. I couldn't imagine going through losing my job if we had kids. I was seeking much more security than that. I needed something solid to secure our financial future, but what? This reflection fuelled my commitment to carve out a new professional journey. One that not only fulfilled my aspirations but also offered stability.

Over the past decade, a select few individuals have sown seeds in my mind, which significantly altered the course of my decision-making journey. Firstly, in that tough year, there were two friends who I consider family, Ann and Rachel, who helped me so much that year and I'll never feel I could fully repay their kindness.

Sometimes people help who you don't know. The lady in the job centre was one of them. She pointed out my transferable skills and said I should see a business mentor. She put me in touch with Stephen. He took me to a business networking group where I was trying to promote my social media business. Every week, I attended the business networking meeting. But I still had no clue how to get my business off the ground. A few months later, one of these select individuals planted a seed that changed my life forever. Chris also attended the business networking group. He wanted to show everyone how you could get paid every month for work done once. I got up and started walking down the café's stairs. I wasn't interested in what he had to say. It sounded like a scam. He said, "Lucy, sit down you need to hear this". I sat down and watched the whole presentation. I was so excited that I said I would be at his office to sign up on Monday.

Speculating to accumulate

I had saved £100, and that was all the extra money we had. We were saving for a bed at the time. We were sleeping on blow up mattresses due to moving from a furnished house to an unfurnished flat. I went to his office, gave him £100 cash, and told him this was all the savings I had. He said I better make this work then. I knew so strongly that passive income would offer financial security. I would love to tell you it was a straight road to earning £1000 a month, but it had many challenges. My mindset needed a whole reset to go from an employee mindset to an entrepreneur mindset. Fortunately, I found myself in the optimal environment for personal growth, allowing me to perceive the world not as a realm of challenges but as a realm brimming with opportunities. That world was network marketing. I spent eight years in the same London-based company from 2013 to 2021. I helped over 300 customers save money. It wasn't all plain sailing in the early days; we were really struggling for money. I struggled with rejection when others couldn't see what I could see with this amazing company. I thought, why don't people want to join my team? I must be the most ambitious person I know around here. I would also get very defensive and desperate because I wanted this to work so much. In 2015, I achieved team leader status, which gave me a real boost. I worked on everything that year: my health, my business and my mindset.

Momtrepreneur life

I was going to put motherhood off until everything was perfect. Perfect car, perfect house with a garden and £1000 a month passive income from this business. That way, I could stop working and still get paid whilst being a mum.

Sadly, I got the devastating news that my mum's best friend's daughter had weeks to live. Nicola had a little girl who was just six years old. My mum told me about the news after one of our days out, and I burst into tears and said, "What am I waiting for?" I was waiting for everything to be perfect; that news was one of those life's too-short moments. That was July 2015, and Mike and I found out we were having a baby by September. Our reason why had just got bigger.

I was determined to get the business to over fifty personal customers. This would secure the passive income. It wasn't a massive amount, but we needed every penny with a new baby on the way. In January, I walked across the stage at the company Kick-off event. I received my 50 + certificate and gave a speech about why that was my first goal. By April, I knew I needed to stop working so hard. I was massive and knackered. I got so poorly one evening after signing up a customer that I had to call the doctor. On the 29th of May 2016, Tommy was born weighing 9lb 13 ounces, and just like that, our lives changed forever. Having a child is one of the most humbling experiences that has ever happened to me. It softens you and brings an air of kindness and humility. I even apologised to my sister, who had birthed her daughter when she was 18. My sister was fantastic in those first few weeks, taking me food shopping and out to lunch. Our finances got better because I received maternity pay. Mike was working hard and putting lots of overtime in. But I knew the business was still very small, and the maternity pay would soon vanish in January.

I attended the company event in the September. I prepared a freezer full of breast milk and left a 3-month-old Tommy with his Daddy for the day. I went to the event determined to learn how I could sign all these mums up I'd met at baby groups. I can't remember any of that event. My boobs were so sore as I didn't have Tommy with me, and they were ready to explode on the way home. All I had to look forward to was another dose of mastitis and very little sleep. I felt unbelievable pressure to make our little family financially secure. I made all the mistakes in the network marketing book. I wanted all the mums in the baby group to join my team, but that never happened because I wanted it more than they did.

In January 2017, as if by magic, the company brought in a quick income plan. What this meant was we would get around £250 per customer. But it also meant our passive income on those customers would be on hold for around three years. I only needed two customers a month to make £500. But I was on my knees by the summer with sleep deprivation and felt very time-poor. It would have been easier to put Tommy in a nursery and go and sit at a supermarket checkout. But what would have been the point? The majority of my wages would have gone to childcare anyway. So, I pushed on with my business.

Achieving big goals

In January 2018, I attended a two-day training with two company leaders who asked me a question I'll never forget. We were all having dinner that evening and a few glasses of wine. One of the leaders asked me, "Lucy, what's your biggest goal this year?" My answer was, "I need my house". We were living in a two-bedroomed upstairs flat. I was so sick of being unable to push Tommy's pushchair straight through the front door. Plus, owning our own home with a garden was my number one goal. As soon as I came home from that event, I knew I needed to take action.

We knew that Mike's parents wanted to move to a nearby village, and I knew which part they wanted to be in. I went armed with 25 flyers I printed at the library, and they read: - "Are you looking to sell your home, cash buyers interested, phone Lucy on this number." I knew that everything was a numbers game and always based my ratios on 1 in 10. Therefore, I knew at least two people would contact me, and they did. I had no idea how we would buy Mike's parents' home. I knew we had enough saved to cover solicitors' fees but not enough for a deposit.

My mum taught me the biggest lesson I've ever learned when I failed my A levels. "Lucy, there's always more than one way to skin a cat". That's Cumbrian, for there's always a way to get what you want. I will never forget her saying that, and I apply it to everything I do now. I rang a local building society for a valuation on my in-law's home. I said to the woman on the phone, I've no deposit, so I still don't know how we are going to do this. She then explained to me about equity deposits which I'd never heard of before. By April, we had completed it. We moved house in May 2018. Mike was two when he moved into the house in 1982, and Tommy was almost two when he moved in.

2018 was one of my best years in business. I won regional awards for customer gatherings. By 2019, I qualified for our first family holiday, all expenses paid, and a company car with all the branding. By 2020, I qualified for another one; by 2021, I had qualified for two-weekend breaks.

Feeling stuck

But my team wasn't growing enough to get the £1k a month passive income I desired. I watched countless people walk across the stage and achieve the next rank level. I couldn't be happy for them because I wanted it so badly it would leave me in tears. In the winter lockdown of 2021, my whole team had gone into what they call witness protection. They weren't responding to my messages. I signed up two customers by the February and enough to qualify me for the second holiday by the April.

I found winter lockdown the most challenging time ever. I needed some bread for my head, so I decided to do another course, but this time, it was manifesting. I knew I needed to work on my mindset. I was doing two courses every morning, a manifesting one and a business one. Plus, I had four-year-old Tommy to look after on my own for thirteen hours a day as we were in the middle of a lockdown. Every morning, I'd get up early to do the modules. What I didn't realise was I was manifesting myself out of my network marketing business. I remember writing, "I am a senior team leader, and I now earn £1k a month" over and over again. I was telling the universe how I would achieve my income goal and not what the goal was. Now, it would read something like "I am so happy and grateful now that I earn £5k a month".

I've recently investigated Human Design. I worked out that I'm a nonspecific manifester. Although my income goal is specific, the how to get there should be less specific. The how lies in the hands of the universe. I know people who are specific manifesters. Their brains are wired very differently to mine. One of these is now a good friend, and she changed my business journey for good.

Finding my tribe

It was April 2021, and the world was slowly starting to wake up again. I met up with two of my team members to watch the company event. Due to the lockdown, it was being live-streamed. I had never felt so flat after watching it. Things had changed in that company, and so had I.

I posted on our local Mums in Business group seeking some help. "Tired, frustrated & emotional, usually holding it together, but tonight I've had enough of trying so hard." I was totally burnt out. I spent the whole day sitting on the bed until it was time for Tommy to come home from Nana's house. I looked at my phone, and I had received a voice note from a lady called Kirsty. She and my husband used to work together years ago. She was concerned about me and contacted me to see what was happening. I explained to her how bad it had gotten with the business. I couldn't see how I was going to make it work. Talking to her was like night and day. She was very successful in her beauty and wellness company and having fun in the process. Success leaves clues. How she was building her business was the complete opposite of how I was building mine. I couldn't believe how much more positive she sounded. She shared many tips on what I could do to grow my team. One day, she said, "I know you're going to say no, but why don't you have a look at what I'm doing?" I had always said I'd never do product sales as I couldn't see how products would make you a true passive income.

I said no to Kirsty for about six weeks until June 2021. I did the unspeakable by changing network marketing companies. Working in that team was so much fun, and everyone wanted to be part of our upline Sharlie and Natasha's team. More importantly, I was surrounded by mums like me who knew how to fit the business around their families.

I worked 2-3 hours daily on that business and made a good income. I had lots of time to spend with Tommy and Mike as my evenings weren't taken up by appointments. Mike and I had also made the decision to take Tommy out of school to home-educate him, which felt like jumping off a cliff. Politically, we did not like what we were seeing in the world. That meant we did not want our son to be part of that system.

Pivoting from head to heart

Another year, another hurdle. In January 2022, our upline decided to change companies. Kirsty and I joined under Sharlie in another company but lost the excitement. No experiences are ever wasted, and what I learned from those ladies has helped with my new business. 2022 was the year I went from head to heart and started writing my first book whilst educating Tommy at home.

I'd always loved Christmas crafts, cooking and decorating. I also loved planning Christmas. I had countless Christmas lists in my phone. That January, I decided to compile these lists into a book. That book is now called 'Christmas Made Easy' and can be purchased on Amazon. It took me ten months and around two hours, most early mornings before Tommy would wake up to finish that book. I launched Christmas Made Easy in October 2022. I loved relearning page design skills from studying journalism. Finally, after fourteen years, I was using my degree. But I soon learned one book alone wasn't the road to riches. In the September I joined a Facebook group. Kirsty had seen it advertised.

I joined up in September 2022 so I could really focus on making the book and my brand a success. I then decided I wanted to design my own planner. 'Chaos to Calm', a planner for mums, was launched in March 2023. Yet again, another seed was planted in my brain, which has helped expand the business. I met a lovely lady called Carol through that network. She suggested I could take parts of the planner and market them as individual planners. One planner became 5, then 25 plus bundles.

Get Organised with Lucy was born

In April 2023, I set up my Etsy store. I started to design planners for mums to help guide them from chaos to calm. Designing planners and writing my book have been the first two roles ever that haven't felt like hard work. I love writing and designing pages and seeing it all come together. I'm forty this year, and I've finally found what I want to do when I grow up. My planners include a gardening planner, a fitness planner, a Christmas planner and a goal-getting planner, to mention a few.

More recently, I have been designing activity books mums can do with their children. My winter solstice planner has been my best-selling item so far. There will be an activity book for every holiday of the year coming soon.

I also run a free Facebook group for mums under Get Organised with Lucy. Each month, I have a guest speaker come and share tips. There have been over 20 women who contributed to the guest speaker slots, and there's more to come. We have had topics on cleaning, time management, fitness, and cyclical living. These lives will be for everyone to enjoy now on my Facebook profile page, Lucy Foster Paterson, to reach a wider audience. Members who join the group and mailing list receive a free, organised five-day course in their email. Plus, there is the option to purchase my Get Organised course if they want a more in-depth version.

I knew I wanted a business that came from the heart with affordable products for all mums. I never wanted another mum to feel as down on herself as I felt in those early years of motherhood. The battle between the mother and the woman inside us can be so overwhelming. My intention is that my products can help mums make peace with those two sides of themselves. Plus, it helps to ditch the mum's guilt for good. I've created an incredible business working from home around my family. It's been hard, and it's been fun and a massive learning curve.

I now want you to borrow my belief that you can achieve whatever makes your heart sing alongside a life that works for you and your family. Whether you need physical tools to help you get organised or simply want a supportive community of mums, I invite you to connect with me through Facebook, where I share valuable insights, host guest speakers, and foster a community of empowered mums.

Dive into my products, from goal-getting planners to engaging children's activity books designed for home educators and school holiday fun. Click on my Linktr.ee below for planners, books, courses and community and navigate your way to a more empowered and organised lifestyle.

All my links - Lucy Paterson | Instagram, Facebook | Linktree
Etsy store: www.getorganisedwithlucy.etsy.com
My Free five-day organising course and Facebook group access:
www.facebook.com/groups/616531399489375/

I look forward to connecting with you on Facebook or Instagram soon.

Best wishes, Lucy x

CHAPTER 6
Laura Crosby

Creator of LDesigns Creations – Home of Life Track Planners and Laura Loves Robin Gift Shop.

Child of the 80's

I grew up in the most normal household really. Mum, Dad, and brother in a semi-detached house in the suburbs of a large city. Dad was a bus driver and Mum was a stay-at-home parent who gradually returned to work as we kids got older. It was normal.

We went to the local church where I had a few friends. We had holidays in a caravan. We were comfortable enough, but we had to be sensible with money, even though Mum and Dad worked hard.

I didn't fit in at school. For a start, I didn't have all the new fashions like most of the other kids (I desperately wanted a pair of slouch socks, but they were so expensive!), and even back in the 80s you would be singled out for not being the same as everyone else. Part of me didn't care as I was always creative and, in many ways, I enjoyed being an individual, which included the way I dressed, but sometimes I just wanted to be like the other kids, so I didn't get bullied or ignored. I felt my presence was just tolerated rather than embraced by the others.

When I got to secondary school, fitting in became even more difficult. Despite there being a whole lot of new people to meet because I didn't go to the local secondary with everyone else from my primary school, the kids at the new school didn't like my individuality and refusal to conform either. I was considered a goody two shoes because I went to church, I was the tallest girl in my class, and I had, what I called, Vampire teeth (long story)! They say you should ignore bullies, but I've always been feisty and tried to stand up for myself, which didn't help me one bit. I spent the rest of my school life feeling unwanted and lonely. I developed severe anxiety around school, making me ill, and it would be hailed a miracle if I managed to attend for a full week without any days off. Despite my absences, I did okay in my GCSEs and for some reason I decided to stay on at the school's Sixth Form. Probably because I thought it might be easier than starting somewhere else with more new people.

For many reasons though, I never finished my A-Levels. I started volunteering in the church instead because at least there I felt accepted and had people who would be nice to me! I even had a long-distance boyfriend after a 'once in a lifetime' trip to Australia with the youth group of the church. He ended up breaking my heart though, and it just added to the deep-seated feelings of rejection I already had.

Eventually, it was time to get myself a job in the 'Real World'. After I got my first proper part-time job, I started to struggle with my health. I was diagnosed with I.B.S. and I was signed off sick. It then became extremely difficult to find another job, and when I did, they always ended abruptly. It wasn't even issues relating to my health really, just workplace politics etc. It brought more feelings of rejection and I started struggling with depression. My physical symptoms were so unpredictable and often came on so suddenly that I would have to change plans or let people down at the last minute. In the end, I gave up trying to work.

I'd started having migraines and was struggling with sciatica, so I had to stop dancing, one of the few activities I was still doing that made me happy. I was married by now, and I did a little bit of book-keeping for him at home instead. I felt almost grateful that I could help contribute to the household income that way, even though it felt like I was doing the bare minimum.

So Why Start a Business?

I just wanted to do something to make a little bit of money. 20 years ago, there weren't the same opportunities to work from home as there are today. Being the creative type, I'd made the invitations for my wedding and even designed my own dress because, once again, I wanted to be unique. So I thought I'd turn that creative flare towards making some money.

Back then, it was hard to sell crafts without attending craft fairs and standing about all day, sometimes in the rain and cold, hoping that somebody... anybody would like your creations enough to actually PAY for them. My biggest customer was my Mum though, and whilst I always appreciated her support, it got me down that no one else I knew (or didn't know) wanted my creations.

I just wanted to make some extra pocket money, but I didn't even manage that. If anything, I spent more on craft supplies than I ever made with the finished products. Being creative, you're often a perfectionist and your own worst critic. The more I didn't sell, the more defeated I felt.

I developed 'Shiny Object Syndrome'. Seeing something and wanting to try it, thinking I could do just as good a job, if not better. This led me to my next attempt at creating a business, Ultimate Nappy cakes. I had bought a nappycake for a friend's baby shower and decided that I could make and sell them for less. Why less? I have no idea. Maybe I was devaluing them because I felt like nobody would buy from me, or maybe I thought what I originally bought was overpriced. Either way, it wasn't the best business model! After a few years of trying to sell them at craft fairs, advertising them to local children's nurseries and even building myself a free website, I was getting nowhere with it. I had a few regular customers but nothing that would give me an income to speak of. Hardly anyone I knew ordered from me, despite them knowing what I was doing, and a baby boom was happening around me at the time. Yet more feelings of rejection.

I decided that I needed to invest in it and get serious. I paid for a professional website (which was a waste of money in many respects), got myself a Facebook page and tried boosting a few posts, all to no avail. If I'm brutally honest with myself, I'm not even the biggest fan of making nappy cakes. Though I'm quite good at it, they're a pain to make and deliver. But I carried on regardless because I didn't know what else to do, and if you asked me now, I would probably still make one for you because I'm a major people pleaser!

I was determined to make it work, but I had no clue how to make it happen. I thought if you had a nice website and a Facebook page it would bring in the orders, but of course it didn't.

Now What?

Despite not making any real progress, I found that I was stuck in the mindset of, "If I build it, they will come". I hit 40 and got a new digital cutting machine (yet another shiny object)! I started making more crafts, but again, I was stuck doing craft fairs with the new products I created, and the income was completely hit and miss. I started an Etsy shop but wasn't even listing much on there. Why? It just felt like a lot of work! How was I ever going to make money with an attitude like that? Forget "If they build it", I was barely digging the foundations for a successful business. Let alone building any walls.

Covid had hit the year before my 40th, and strangely, out of the blue, I found myself a job. I managed to do my new job quite successfully as I was only required to do a few hours a week, and more often than not, I had the flexibility to decide when I would work. Sometimes it was a struggle, especially the more physical aspects of the job and more than once I would have to sort out issues when I was not feeling my best.

I found that I could manage more than I realised though, and it built my confidence up again. I was doing such a good job that I even started getting commissions for the bookings I brought in. Sadly, the job ended quite suddenly, and I was devastated as I was getting used to finally being able to pay my own way a little, as well as getting to talk to people instead of constantly being home alone. It hit me hard. After this, my health started playing up again.

I became pre-diabetic, so I had to start monitoring my diet, exercise and weight, which did nothing for my self-esteem. I was diagnosed as fructose intolerant, which makes healthy eating a real challenge because fruit and vegetables become your mortal enemy, and I was having problems with my heart rhythm, which caused me to need medication. This all meant my anxiety re-emerged, and I felt really low. Added to the fact that people had disappeared from my life, it was a recipe to make me want to give up because I knew that, financially, I didn't even need to work.

But I was so sick of feeling like I wasn't achieving anything for myself, and I wanted to be financially independent, now that I'd entered my 40's, because you never know what may happen in the future.

Chain of Events

I was never one for giving up though. In fact, I often joke that I'm a little bit Chumbawamba -I get knocked down, but I get up again!

However, I had no idea what to do next when I came across a lovely lady called Mandy Nicholson on Facebook. She helps creative people build a money-making business using their creative talents. Her story was so inspiring, it made me realise that just because life isn't great right now, it doesn't mean that it can't get better, and no matter what has happened before, you can start again.

I attended her five-day course, and it renewed my energy for wanting to make my own creative business work. However, where it led me next was going to be the biggest leap forward in my journey so far. Mandy was asked to speak at the Facebook launch of a new online platform for entrepreneurs, giving support and real-world training to help people build a successful business. I attended because of Mandy, but by the second day of the week's launch, I was thinking that this was where I needed to be. By the fourth day, I had signed up, and I haven't looked back since.

During this time, I was finding it really difficult to keep on top of all my health issues though, both mental and physical, as well as my everyday life. I wanted a diary to keep all the important information in one place, but I couldn't find anything suitable. Through the online training, I learned that I could make my own planner/diary using Amazon KDP for no initial outlay.

Then I started thinking about how many other people there must be out there who are dealing with the same sort of health issues and finding it hard to keep track of it all. So I started designing the planner. I shared the idea with a new friend of mine whom I met at a networking event. She specialises in courses for mindfulness and self-care (which I attended and got so much out of) and is particularly well-versed in the body-mind connection. She thought the planner was a great idea which boosted my confidence to do it. As did attending the networking events. I have always been shy around new people, and I had to really shift my mindset of nobody liking me just to have the guts to attend.

But I swallowed the fear, realising that I needed to get myself out there and make new connections. I'm so glad I did, it turned out some people do and will like me for me! However, I was still filled with self-doubt about my new idea. Thinking, "Why would anyone buy from me? They never have in the past. Nobody wants what I make, and I clearly don't have the skills to convince them otherwise. I've failed in creating my own business before so what makes me think I can do it now? It must be perfect because otherwise people will criticise it and I'll be straight back to believing that I'm useless." How on earth do I push past the negativity and finally publish my idea? By not listening to the Monkey Circus (as my friend Carole calls it)! The thoughts that aren't even true, but we constantly tell ourselves. Overthinking everything when we should just get on with it! So, if those thoughts do start going around in your head, do it anyway like I did! Fill your head with positive affirmations, learn what you don't know and get support from those around you. You might still feel like you can't, but feel the fear and do it anyway. The more you achieve, the more confidence you'll have in yourself, your business, and your life. Even the smallest achievements can give you a massive boost. The realisation that my planners can help more people than just myself keeps me motivated. There are people out there, like me, who struggle with their own health issues. How can I not try to help when I know the sort of things they go through every day? I had to try, so I got out of my own way and clicked 'Publish'!

Life Track Planners are now on Amazon.

I've also created my own website with the help of Tracey. I was struggling to do it on my own as the technology had advanced so far since my last attempt. However, with help, I have managed to create a website that I'm proud for people to visit. Amanda has also been so encouraging, and her sessions have been a big part of getting some self-belief back.

I still get to use my creativity, which I love, and I've also started to build up my Etsy shop, Laura Loves Robin, where I now sell Print on Demand products, many of which have positive messages at their heart as I want to spread joy, especially to people who may not be in a particularly positive mindset, because I know how it feels.

Carry on Regardless!

Despite still working from home, I now have a new group of supporters that I never expected to have. There are so many inspirational stories from other students and teachers on the entrepreneurs training platform who have started from scratch and created something successful despite any challenges. It gives me the encouragement that I can do the same. Even though I struggle to share and be as open as many others in the group (another mindset I am still working on), I try to be as helpful in the group as possible. It's amazing just to feel like you can be useful and encourage others on the same journey as you. I no longer feel like I'm on this journey alone, and I've learnt so much more about business and mindset than I ever have before. I'm still working on being less alone in my personal world, overcoming the feelings that nobody will accept me the way I am because that's how it's been in the past, but I'm getting there and becoming more like my happier, cheeky and slightly feisty self again. I'm the first to admit that I'm not necessarily moving forward as fast as I would like. However, I am trying to make a little progress every day, doing one step at a time. As one of the founders of the entrepreneurs training platform once said, "It is far better to move slowly in the right direction, than to move quickly in the wrong direction."

I hold onto this mindset. Even when I'm too ill to work on my business, I'm still thinking what the next step is for me to take. I'm always coming up with ideas, and my 'Shiny Object Syndrome' often still runs riot, but I try to embrace it now. After all, the more ideas you have, the more options you have for creating a successful business!

A lot of stories you hear these days are the ones where people have sudden, dramatic shifts in their mindset to become all they could be, and they're inspiring to hear. But sometimes, the story is about doing something despite your own mindset, and that's me. I have to deal with procrastination, confusion and a lack of confidence almost daily. I still feel like I don't have a clue what I'm doing a lot of the time.

These businesses are a world away from anything I've done before, and it's more exposing in many ways because it stems from my own personal journey struggling with my physical and mental health. This is also a massive mindset shift, as I've always been taught that your private life should always be private so I still fear being judged. I was even hesitant about writing a chapter for this book. But if something I share can help others, then why wouldn't I?

I have to remind myself that people don't always understand what you're doing or why you're doing it, especially when you've grown up thinking that the 9-5 grind is the way you make money and entrepreneurship is only for the likes of Bill Gates, Richard Branson and the Dragons in Dragons Den. This is a belief I carried myself for many years, and despite my health not giving me a lot of choice in the matter, it took a long time to stop feeling like I wasn't achieving anything in life because I didn't have a 'proper job' like everyone else.

I've learned that in order to be an entrepreneur, you must develop a growth mindset. Looking at what does and doesn't work and adapt accordingly. Is this easy for me? No way! I'm still a complete beginner when it comes to breaking the fixed mindsets and feelings from the past that hold me back. However, I am now a firm believer that you just have to keep going on the path you're building for yourself and tackle your mindset as you go along. Find the help and support when you need it and try to ignore those who just don't get it. One of the biggest realities that I've faced in recent years is trying to understand that you are only in charge of your own thoughts and actions and you have to leave everyone else to deal with theirs, even if it's hard to do because we want people to approve of us so much.

Life Track Planners and Laura Loves Robin are still in their infancy, but I have so many ideas for how they can help people in different ways whilst also trying to bring a little joy into their lives. I am still working on my own mindset every day in order to progress, and I know I've still got a lot to learn on the practical side. But I'm doing it, slowly and surely, despite any negative thoughts that rear their ugly heads, whether they're my own or other people's.

As Mark Twain once said, "The secret to getting ahead is getting started." I am just getting started, and I can't wait to see where this path will take me!

If you'd like to find out more about my planners or know someone you think may benefit from them, please visit my website where you can sign up for a free planner page as well as all the latest from Life Track Planners and Laura Loves Robin.

Website: www.lifetrackplanners.co.uk
Etsy: www.lauralovesrobin.etsy.com
Facebook: www.facebook.com/lifetrackplanners
Facebook: www.facebook.com/lauralovesrobin
Instagram: www.instagram.com/ldesignscreations
Linktr.ee: www.linktr.ee/ldesignscreations

CHAPTER 7

Annemarie Farrow

Female Life and Wellbeing Coach

My name is Annemarie, I am 48 and I am currently working as a mental health nurse and will move from the nursing space to the wellbeing coaching space this year. That is not where my journey started but this is where the last 30 years have taken my life and career. Let's journey back to the starting point, where my passion and commitment to making a difference first started.

I was born in the summer of 1975 in the local hospital, to a young mum and dad. We lived in a council flat across the road from my paternal grandparents for 10 years thereabout.

My brother was born in the winter of 1978. I do not recall much of my childhood, not because it was an unhappy childhood, it wasn't- I just do not recall most of it. My recollection of the past 30 years is quite sketchy, to say the least, other than moving a few times from house to house and settling when I was a teenager in the Village of Garelochhead with my family. By the time we moved to Garelochhead, my mum had divorced my dad and remarried a Welsh submariner, and my sisters were born in 1986- they are twins.

Whilst living in Garelochhead, I left high school at 17 and started on a government Youth Training Scheme. It was in an office, which I hated. I would travel from Garelochhead to Dumbarton on the local bus, which seemed like it was taking days over an hour in reality. This gave me enough time to realise I don't want to work for anyone else but myself in the future. I worked this job Monday-Friday 9 am-5 pm for £42 a week. Unbeknown to me at the age of 17, this would be the start of a 30-year working life as an employee, where I simply never felt like I belonged.

I left school with few qualifications I had failed maths (I still cannot do any maths, or arithmetic to this day, I need to use the calculator on my phone) and I did not even get a grade for modern studies the paper must have been that poor. I didn't enjoy school or learning at that time, I found the academic road difficult and still do, I don't feel I am particularly smart.

After leaving the YTS, I went on to attend college in Greenock for the next 3 years studying Social Sciences. The thought behind this was to go on and qualify as a clinical psychologist and work in the forensic services, as the way people think and their subsequent behaviour patterns have always fascinated me, why do people behave the way they do, and say the things they say? Well, that is not the road I travelled.

My first "real" job was working for the Department of Work & Pensions where over my 17 years there, I met some of the most incredible people and they have stayed friends throughout my adult life. Most notably the person I consider to be my best friend, Irene-we have been friends for over 30 years and in that time-life has changed beyond recognition for both of us. I got married and divorced after more than 20 years-became single for the first time in my life in my late 30s, lived in my sisters' spare room for a year whilst navigating a divorce and having no idea where this thing called life was going to take me.

That old familiar feeling

I have always been blessed (it is a blessing, I think) with a deep spiritual connection, I believe there is something after this life, I believe we are guided by "something", I believe truly when a door closes, the window opens we just need to find the courage to climb through the window. I am an empath by character and can feel everything that someone else feels and feel my feelings quite acutely think it's why people gravitate to me naturally and tell me their life story without blinking an eye. When these situations occur-they are always followed up by "I have no idea why I just told you all that! I've never told anyone that before".

I can also feel instinctively when I need to move on, it doesn't matter what I am moving on from, a job/service or a relationship. I get a very deep unshakable unsettled feeling and it simply grows if I do not reflect and then act on it. That feeling presents itself as anxiety and low confidence, I question my decisions, struggle to sleep, and begin to overthink then require external validation that the decision I'm making is the right one for me!!!!! This feeling becomes very strong over time and simply stays as a feeling until I address it.

I have learned over the past 30 years not to ignore this feeling and now, I lean into it and wonder where the next journey will take me. Often, I have not planned for a change it just happens I do not plan anything, I trust the process and let the tapestry unfold, a bit risky some might say! I have often been asked "Why can't you just conform

Annemarie and stay in a job" I've had statements like "No one likes their job, but we can't keep moving around." and "We only work Monday to Friday, why can't you have your life on a Saturday and Sunday like everyone else"-no thanks I want to live my life all week-not around a job.

I remember distinctly the day I decided to leave DWP for my next chapter, it was January 2009, and January in Scotland, It was freezing, wet and dark, I was driving to work and said aloud to myself "This is the last year I'm doing this job"-and it was! As I worked at DWP, I also studied BSc in Psychology over 4 years through the Open University. I graduated with a 2:2 honours degree and did absolutely nothing with it, the certificate lived in a cheap A4 ring binder, and it still lives in that ring binder now, with many other qualifications I have achieved throughout my life.

I continued working in DWP for another 10 years after university, having also been certified as a Reiki practitioner and studying massage equally did not put any of this to effective use. As we go on, you will see I am a serial learner and I have just learned I do not "learn & do"-I learn, learn and learn have often wondered why I never follow up with action or a change in direction, like starting a business for myself? I think on reflection, it has been because I have conformed to the employee mindset for over 30 years, it is safe, protective and comfortable.

In the blink of an eye

I studied Mental Health Nursing at the University of West of Scotland from 2009-2012, this was the path I took after that dark, cold day driving to work. I graduated with distinction and started my nursing career. Although, I do remember in my second year feeling that old familiar feeling and having thoughts of - I'm not sure this is for you this is the one time I completely ignored my intuition and all these years later I still do not know why I did that, although I have my suspicions, it was to lead me on the path I'm taking now.

Being a newly qualified mental health nurse, I had grown academically, and spiritually and in many ways had grown away from the life I had once lived and thought I loved. After many years of trying to make a marriage work, that simply didn't work, I moved out of the marital home and brought an end to my marriage. I lived in the spare room of my younger sister with her and her husband for a year. I will be eternally grateful for the kindness they offered me at that confusing and isolating time.

I worked full-time and had to continue to pay the bills for my marital home, I had naively put all the bills in my name over the years. It took a year to buy my home back from my ex-husband and I was left with thousands of pounds worth of a loan to leave that marriage. This was a very testing time in my life and my overthinking and anxious nature made me wonder why I had failed at this marriage. Little did I know, at one of the most testing points of my life-the universe was just waiting in the wings to deliver everything I've ever dreamed of!

By the end of my marriage, I had moved jobs (again!) had left nursing and had taken up a post as a Care Manager for a local home care company. The owner offered a salary of £11,000 higher than my NHS post. I decided to leave the NHS and leap into the private sector and see where that chapter took me. This was my first leap of faith really in myself, with no sick pay, and no private pension offers at that time, but I loved this job; I did this for 4 years before coming back into the NHS as I felt, you guessed it, that old familiar feeling.

And then, my beloved uncle Paul died suddenly and in the blink of an eye, he was no longer here. No more parties, late-night chats, impromptu get-togethers, laughing or arguing, mostly about politics! No more after-life discussions, where do we go after, who do we meet when we get there? Just a massive, void that will never close over until the day I die. Nearly eight years on, the impact of his departure is as acute as that day. It was also the event that changed my life, Thoughts of being my own boss grew stronger, I didn't want to be an employee to ask to take time off work to spend time with loved ones or ask for holidays or get promotions to get a decent salary anymore. So since then, I have quietly worked in the background with self-employment as a goal.

I have also failed at two self-employment opportunities I realise they didn't set my soul on fire, I didn't have an interest, just a desperation to be my own boss.

Since that awful day in 2016, I have felt that old familiar feeling more often than ever!! I have studied and certified in many other topics and put the certificates in the ring binder. Having no idea how to start a business for myself I told myself "Maybe self-employment is not the right route for you" "I bet you couldn't set up for yourself anyway", "What do you know about business" is my favourite self-limiting belief that I've had to work hard on quieting down. So, I continue to nurse in the NHS with the burning desire to launch into business for myself.

Nursing, menopause & burnout

I returned to the NHS and worked on a ward with elderly patients, another role that brought me great joy, after the pain of my uncle's death. The simple task of helping someone shower, dress, eat and drink, is such a privilege I felt and still feel. When you are at your most vulnerable, what is it you want to feel? I think it's safe, looked after and loved. Until again, that old familiar feeling was starting to surface and after some great shifts and great friendships, I moved from the inpatient setting to a community setting, to a role I knew nothing about. I have always believed in the power of your thoughts and the importance of how you speak to yourself, so I just said "Annemarie, you will learn how to do this job" then did it.

I started that job, not knowing the service and not knowing any of my new colleagues. I spent in all 4 years in that team (leaving once for 6 months to another team after a promotion and then coming back) where I learned more than I ever taught. I learned the importance of connection, trust and belief in your colleagues and them in you. I learned that even in your worst moments, with the right people around you, you will get through it. The colleagues in this team have evolved over the past 7 years to be my very best friends, and then...................

I moved on from this role into a role I never thought I would do, Community Psychiatric Nurse. It turns out, this is the job that taught me EVERYTHING about me! I learned that I am a highly anxious person and like familiarity and comfort zones, this is not what other people see. I have learned I do not feel I fit into the nursing role although I care about people and how they live their lives. I have learned I DO care what other people think and after a lifetime of thinking I lived life on my terms, this has been my most shocking discovery of myself. I have learned I don't feel I am enough, know enough or am smart enough to continue up the promotion ladder, so I don't apply for further promotions.

This was the mindset that led me to the decision to leave patient care, as I felt constantly anxious, low in mood, tearful and irritable, low in motivation, constantly questioned my decision making, compared myself to other nurses, could not sleep and was overeating and putting weight on. I was also setting standards way too high for me to be able to achieve in my work and personal life. I was socially withdrawing and did not want to be anywhere other than my home. It was a chore going to work like never before.

Unbeknown to me at the time I was experiencing burnout. Watching STV news after work, the reporter was describing workplace burnout in the NHS (this was at the time of the Covid 19 pandemic) that news report changed my work direction, it was then I realised I experienced every symptom and started researching burnout. I discussed burnout with the GP trainee, who was studying menopause at the time and advised my further symptom descriptions were perimenopause! YAY! A great combination.

My journey through menopause and HRT continue. I have increased my meditation, journaling and mood board practice to get through.

The road ahead

The job changes, the marriage ending, going to university, twice, the death of my uncle, the birth of my niece in the pandemic, watching my mother's strength in supporting me after her beloved brother's death, taking a leap of faith and investing £5000 to retrain as a wellbeing coach has led me to the present moment. I have always believed the universe has my back-I have no proof of this other than when I jump, I never fall, I always land standing up. That doesn't mean it's not scary, or that I don't have to work hard or give 100 per cent, or that I wouldn't rather sometimes stay in my comfort zone and stick to what I know. It just means, my mindset is now one that I trust in me, and the evidence suggests I can do whatever I believe I can do.

I've also met my now husband 10 years ago and married him two years ago. I have married my soul mate, he grounds me, supports me, scolds me and loves me with every flaw and challenge I present to him and I've brought the menopause into his life!! It is because of his support and unwavering faith in me, that I have been able to move job roles and experience more in my nursing career, I've experienced different services, teams and roles in my work. He believes truly and deeply that I can do anything I put my mind to, I can achieve absolutely anything.

He trusts me 100 per cent with all my decision-making, all my risk-taking, moving jobs and when I get that old familiar feeling of there's more I need to learn, there's other things I need to do, some see it is flighty, some see it as unsettled, some even see it and have voiced it-that they would hate to be like me and never settled, he is right behind me and my biggest cheerleader. He has been in his job for 30 years and has told me, don't ever settle like I did whatever your heart desires-the world needs to know you exist!

It is because of him, that I have spent 2023 working with a Coaching Academy to certify in Money Mindset Transformation, Self-Love and Confidence Building and Menopause Wellness Practice. I will be moving on to the Neuro-Linguistic Programming certification in 2024. I now have the basis of a coaching business and at the time of writing this, I have employed someone to build my coaching website amongst other things and now a business feels in reach. I have employed a business coach and learned more about mindset and goal setting and to think big, then set my goals to align with my vision for the future.

2024 is going to be the year where everything that I have thought of, felt, and visualised will manifest into being. I won't play small any longer to conform to the world narrative, you go to work, save money, have your one holiday a year, and then start all over again. I will make it my mission to help women gain clarity on their limiting beliefs in the areas of their lives that are holding them back and empower them to cultivate self-love, confidence and resilience. I will help women move confidently into the next chapter of their lives with focus. I will also be focusing on writing an online course teaching women effective strategies on how to recover from burnout.

I will leave you with this quote by Henry Ford that I think is a definitive statement of the power of how you think. My philosophy is, that your longest relationship in your life is with yourself, so talk to yourself kindly, be present in your own life, cut yourself some slack, and decide what you want to do to enhance your own life, and in turn, you will enhance the lives of others around you.

So as Henry said, *"whether you think you can, or you think you can't? Either way, you're right".*

I would love to connect with you and find out how I can support you moving through your own life's journey. Please feel free to reach out to me through the link/QR Code below.

Linktree: www.linktr.ee/annemariefarrowwellbeingcoach
Mobile: 07436489877

CHAPTER 8

Julie Hollins

Owner & and Photographer at Julie Hollins Photography

Rising Through Resilience - A Photographic Journey Framing My Journey

Have you ever been in a position where you have a deep-rooted passion and a business idea but never got it off the ground, or maybe started a business and then stopped? Was something holding you back?

Maybe this was because of what people may think, your own limiting beliefs or lack of confidence, or you are just stuck, not being able to move forward, and then BOOM, either God or the Universe (whatever your beliefs) pops something into your path to release you from that place and inch you forward. However, we must be brave enough to receive and act on it to grow and progress. My passion is photography, and this is my story.

My love and fascination for photography trace back to my early years, flipping through photo albums with my Mum over and over. The textured pages and photo hinges holding memories in place – it's a nostalgic scene for those who remember the cardboard photo albums. Oh, what great memories! These were taken with a box camera, which I found fascinating, and it was a cherished moment when I got to capture images myself.

My first camera was given to me by my Mum. It was a disposable camera, and I was on a trip to Versailles, France, at the tender age of 14, to stay with an exchange pen friend. I was limited to 20 images in the camera to capture my 3-week experience. The photos I snapped were the proudest moments capturing the awe of Versailles Palace, the Eiffel Tower, and the joyous moments with the family I was staying with. Over the years, my photography evolved, capturing personal travel experiences alongside a corporate consultancy career travelling nationally and internationally.

A move to South Africa became a new chapter, where, under the guidance of an inspirational photography coach, I realised I could turn my passion into a livelihood. I took up wildlife photography while travelling in Namibia and street photography, which brought great joy, while my business side involved school shoots, and kids' parties (quite a different type of wildlife! They move at the most unexpected moment, which produces the most candid shots.), portraits, and family photography in the most beautiful natural light.

After running my business for about a year, circumstances led me back to England with my young daughter. I ventured into establishing my photography business, opting for a school photography franchise. It soon became apparent that the financial and logistical challenges were not aligning with my mission, values and goals, especially with a little one in tow.

With a heavy heart, I made the difficult decision to close down my photography business and sell my equipment. The entire process felt like saying goodbye to a part of myself, and even the buyer picked up on my hesitation, sensing that letting go wasn't easy for me. Although I continued taking photos for personal enjoyment on my phone and a 'point and shoot' digital camera, it couldn't quite fill the void that selling my equipment had left.

Eventually, I made the shift back into the workforce, this time finding my place in the domain of SMEs (Small to Medium-sized enterprises). On reflection, the decision to close the business was more rooted in the fear of success and lack of self-belief, and had I received the right support and guidance, I now believe it could have thrived.

Embracing Opportunity

Recently, I lost my purpose a little, I wasn't feeling fulfilled, I felt like I was surviving, not thriving. I had some work and life challenges that I was navigating and needed to do something about it as I was feeling particularly low. I needed to do something to uplift me, bring me joy, and shine a light, life is too short. The first thing that came to mind was that it was time to revive my love for photography.

At this point, I wasn't necessarily thinking of earning a second income, although it would be a bonus given the ol' economy at the moment and the likelihood I am going to work forever!! I felt trapped though. I knew what I wanted to do, but I wasn't able to move the needle forward. Where would I even start? I was anxious and had minimal time available, or so I thought, to investigate or pursue it, given my full-time job.

I only had evenings and weekends to follow my dream. How would I be able to do this? I needed some moral support if I was to pick up my camera again. Hold on!! I didn't even have a camera at this point!! And I hadn't prepared myself for what lay ahead.

Then, the 'BOOM' inspiration arrived in my Facebook feed. It was a free, yes free, 5-day mini challenge for the Business of Brand Photography (a business and marketing course for photographers). I dared myself to dream. What the heck! What did I have to lose? What's brand photography? I just registered the word 'photography' in my head and pounced!

My passion is photography, and what I didn't realise when I was stuck in that place was that I could revive and expand my photography services together with my business knowledge and skill set to help small businesses achieve their mission, vision, and goals through creative imagery and business and marketing guidance. 'BOOM' indeed!! Overwhelm had crowded my mind, but when I opened it up to possibilities, there was my opportunity.

There was so much content in such a short but intensive course, that I could have kick-started my business there and then. So what was stopping me? The next few months passed by, and I revisited the course a couple of times and worked out what I needed to set the business up again and get systems in place, never mind all of the targeted marketing. But I just wasn't moving the dial; I was procrastinating. I became anxious because I was thinking that this wasn't going to be possible. Where was I going to find the time? Can I actually do this? But I wanted it so much! And then 'BOOM', what was going on? This can't be happening? God or the Universe has my back, another 5-day mini course dropped into my Facebook feed.

It was specific coaching on shaking anxieties and sabotaging behaviour that stops you from achieving your personal and business goals and dreams. This was the personal guidance that I needed to open my mind further to learn more about myself, and this opportunity and was pivotal to my business growth, confidence, and personal development. This was just what I needed to help me come unstuck.

These programmes were amazing, offering live coaching and Q&A sessions, along with supporting workbooks, and assignments. It felt as if I had stepped into a university-like environment, gaining valuable knowledge and guidance. The coaches and the community were incredibly supportive and encouraging, genuinely invested in seeing everyone thrive in both life and business. It felt like I had discovered my tribe. Being recognised for engagement in the courses was a significant boost. After all, there's no point in taking the courses if you're not going to actively participate – this recognition not only felt great but also motivated me to keep going.

These were the 'BOOM' moments that propelled me past my barriers, affirming that I can indeed achieve it. You have to embrace opportunities…say 'Yes', and work the 'how' out later. The plan was to rekindle my love for photography and expand my services by integrating it with my business and marketing expertise, helping small business owners become more visible to their ideal clients through compelling visual imagery and targeted marketing strategies. I wasn't blinkered, it's not plain sailing, it has to be said that it's important to acknowledge that success doesn't come without hard work and challenges.

From Stoicism to Authenticity

Given the limited time I had available, the challenge was not knowing how to set up the business but rather how to set it up for success. My head was filled with ideas, but the lack of time, guidance, direction, reassurance, and minimal support, with some people thinking I was nuts, made the journey daunting and the end goal a million miles away. I started haphazardly looking into courses without clear objectives, hesitating to begin as they didn't feel right, realising I hadn't selected the right ones.

Some internal challenges that were present at this time were playing with my mind and hindering my ability to break free of myself and pursue what my heart truly desired. The one thing I knew was that I needed to do something to change the way I felt, prompting me to pause and reflect on my aspirations. It became clear that to be the authentic version of myself I needed to shift away from being stoic and internalising everything, a draining pattern I had fallen into. Little did I know I was heading for a huge mindset shift to move forward.

My confidence had taken a bit of a dive; I had tucked it away for safekeeping, fearing success and not knowing what needed to be done to kick-start the process and work through this fear of the unknown. The decision to let go of my photography business in the past, not once but twice, planted the seeds of this fear. The idea of reopening Pandora's box at this point brought some apprehension, as I considered the potential outcomes with feelings of uncertainty.

The crucial aspect was ensuring I could continue providing for my daughter and myself and free myself from the limiting belief that success wasn't for me. To continue to do that, I would have to balance this process with my full-time job, aiming to grow from there. Despite knowing that I could do this, stepping out of my well-established comfort zone posed a challenge. I had firmly rooted myself in a safe place that was delaying my progress and stopping me from moving forward. To feel confident, I first needed to find courage.

Then there was also the tiny issue of not having any camera equipment, a pretty significant asset for a photographer! Remember? I sold it! Also, there was no spare cash for spontaneous purchases. What was I thinking?! However, it was my newfound knowledge and confidence and my passion for photography that propelled me forward. I had initiated my photography business a couple of times in the past, only to let it go through life's ups and downs and a lack of self-belief and courage. So, can I do it now? I had to believe I could, and seeking the right help and guidance to acquire the necessary knowledge was crucial.

Earning more than one source of income was becoming more attractive as a bonus (think of all the travelling!!). We never know what is going to happen, and it would be great to have options to fall back on. However, I wanted to do something I enjoy, that lights me up and brings me a sense of self-worth, being valued, and helping others to be successful. So, I began saving for my camera kit, which filled me with excitement with each piece I purchased. I was going to do this, no matter how long it took.

Fitting in the schedule for the 5-day mini-challenges around my day job was a tight squeeze. I would supercharge my day and get up before the sparrows (soooo early!!), stop at the coffee shop on the way to work to wake up with coffee and listen to the live calls. Armed with the coaching advice and the task for the day, I would set off to work and did the task either at lunchtime or in the evenings before the Q&A session in the evening. Traffic permitting, I would arrive home with just enough time to cook food, eat, and slide myself into the education seat. It was exhausting but exhilarating.

Why was it so important for me to have had and overcome these challenges? It boils down to my 'WHY.' It's about believing I can do this and showcasing to my daughter that, regardless of the situations you find yourself in, you can pursue whatever you desire. You can bounce back from setbacks and follow your dreams with the right structure and a supportive community guiding, supporting, and encouraging you. It's not just about personal achievement but also about setting an example for others, especially those close to me.

Empowering Brands Through Visual Storytelling

Reviving my photography business has brought me personal fulfilment and continuing professional growth. I have my mojo back and more importantly, I have diversified my portfolio to include brand photography allowing me to work closely with business owners like you.

It enables me to combine my lifelong passion for photography with a rich tapestry of experiences garnered from collaborating with both corporate giants and smaller and independent treasures. It's more than headshots, it goes beyond mere image capture; it's an immersive experience of education and knowledge sharing. Your success story comes to light through the art of storytelling, enabling you to become more visible to your ideal clients.

Elevating your brand involves showcasing the person/people behind the business in a way that resonates with your audience. Your narrative is the cornerstone of selling your business and establishing a unique identity. Your individuality becomes the distinguishing factor, setting you apart from others in your industry even when your business offers similar products/services to another business.

If you don't feel comfortable behind the camera, I will ensure you feel at ease and help you to enjoy the process and build an unforgettable experience. I can guide you in expressing your story through visual imagery for all of your marketing needs on and offline, ensuring alignment with your values, mission and goals.

Our collaborative efforts result in the creation of a bespoke image collection that narrates the unique story of your brand, making marketing a delightful and effective venture that sets you apart. The focus is not just on showcasing products or services but on presenting you as the face of your brand, recognising that clients remember experiences more vividly than specifics. The ultimate goal is to evoke positive emotions through visual content and storytelling marketing.

Does stepping in front of a camera fill you with dread? Why not try a 'Brand Teaser' shoot where we can get to know each other, you can become familiar with the process and feel more comfortable in front of the camera? Feeling confident, you can then move onto a complete brand experience refreshing throughout the year; maybe marking particular milestones in your business, having seasonal shoots, events and more.

To learn more, send me a direct message using the link below.

Linktree: www.linktr.ee/juliehollins

> *'Knowing what must be done does away with fear.'*
> *Rosa Parks*

Dedication: *To Taylor, you are braver and stronger than you know. Cling to your resilience, courage, and strength as you confidently chase your dreams. Love you to the moon and back, Mama xx*

CHAPTER 9

Aisha Beg

Transformational and Complementary Therapist specialising in Women's Health and Healing

Early Foundations and Formative Years

Business is not in our blood; we are a family of professionals. I heard my parents say. This was the message given to me as a young adult and one I vehemently stuck to for many years until I didn't! This is the story of how I went from someone who wanted to climb the corporate ladder to rejecting that concept and becoming my boss and a business owner.

I was born into a family that had been shaped by the resilience of immigrant parents, inheriting a legacy of strength in the face of adversity and a robust work ethic. My parents, who encountered financial hardships, racism, and various personal challenges upon moving from India to the UK in the late 1960s, remained unwavering in their pursuit of a better life for their children and the family members they left behind. The stories of their struggles were frequently shared during my childhood and formative years, evolving into life lessons that ultimately shaped my character and outlook on how to navigate hardships.

My parents were devout individuals, possessing an unshakable belief in God and a strong faith that served as a foundation in both good and bad times. They had a deep ethical foundation and were disciplined and principled people. They diligently worked to preserve and transmit their cultural heritage and belief system to my brother and me. Their mindset was one marked by courage, forbearance, tenacity, sacrifice, and a profound, nurturing love for their own family as well as others. Ideals that have been instilled in me because of them.

At the age of 13, the Research & Development department that my father worked in relocated to another county. Being the caring man that he was, he decided not to relocate his family, and uproot his children from their environment, and took voluntary redundancy. The next five years would be incredibly challenging for him as he was already in his mid-50s. He made the brave decision to go back to college and upskill his knowledge to adapt to his new situation.

Watching my parents struggle during these five long years was difficult, and it made my brother and I mature rapidly. Both of us worked part-time whilst studying full-time to not be an added burden on our parents.

At the age of 16, my mother had a sudden heart attack that changed our family dynamic once again. Now, my brother and I became carers as she recovered, life's responsibilities kept piling on our shoulders before we were ready for them. Despite all her health conditions, she maintained a positive outlook on life. Making many positive changes to her lifestyle and nutrition to manage her diabetes, high blood pressure, cholesterol, and heart issues. Looking back with the knowledge that I have now, I do believe her illness was rooted in stress, as both her diet and lifestyle were good from a young age. It is true when they say stress is a killer.

My ambitious mindset grew from my parents' teachings and became a driving force within me. A burning desire to excel and become successful despite the odds being stacked against you. The belief that one could achieve anything with determination and a positive attitude laid the foundation for a successful career in Human Resources and Talent Acquisition. Working with prestigious multinational companies on an international level made me see the immense opportunities that were available to me. Each challenge became an opportunity for mindset shifts, fostering resilience that would prove crucial in the chapters yet to unfold in my life.

Pneumonia strikes, stopping me in my tracks

At the age of 25, I was living the dream: married to the love of my life, my career was taking off, and I was dreaming big and working very hard.... A little too hard. Commuting 3-4 hours every day and studying classical Arabic in the evenings, then commuting to Yorkshire to see inlaws at the weekend. Pneumonia hit me like a truck out of nowhere. I was rushed to hospital in an ambulance and hospitalised for ten days. The doctors were shocked at my condition due to my relatively young age and being in good general health, I was not their usual pneumonia case.

After ten long days, I was finally discharged, only to be readmitted with pleurisy a week later. This was another devastating blow. In my mind, I planned to be back at work within a few weeks.

The road to recovery took months. This episode made me realise that I had been pushing myself beyond my limits and the fragility of life, something needed to change. That change was to move from London to Leeds to live a slower-paced life and begin to start a family of our own.

The entrepreneur inside awakens

Not one to sit on my laurels, I decided to become an entrepreneur, and my husband and I set up our own company. Designed our main product and travelled to China to source a factory to produce it. The entrepreneurial life was not linear and had many ups and downs. The learning curve was a steep one, and we realised that working together was not as easy as we had romanticised it to be. Very soon, our business baby turned into a real baby, and we welcomed our firstborn daughter in 2005.

Although the pregnancy was textbook perfect, the labour was completely different and turned what should have been a straightforward delivery into a 36-hour nightmare, ending in an emergency caesarean section. None of which I had imagined on my labour vision board! Once again, I underestimated recovery time. In my mind, I would be back to normal in a couple of months. Motherhood had other plans, and it was a whole year before I felt normal again. Navigating motherhood, exclusive breastfeeding, colic, and a baby who didn't sleep was exhausting and demoralising. Clashes in parenting style and other personal issues took a dramatic turn, and we decided to return to familiar London with a one-year-old and purchase our first home.

We were finally homeowners, and life was bliss for a short while until redundancy hit once again. At this point, we decided that we would consider all available options open to us as the UK was entering a financial crisis. This mindset shift took us halfway across the world to the UAE where we embarked on a new adventure that would last six years and would see our family grow and flourish.

Changing Continents: A Leap of Faith to the UAE

My husband left for the UAE to start his new job, and my daughter and I joined him a month later. Packing up all our belongings and moving away from family was not an easy decision to make. We were embarking on a new life many thousands of miles away, leaving behind family, friends, familiarity, and the country we had roots in. Together, we faced the daunting task of starting anew.

The UAE quickly became our home, which we loved. A beautiful canvas for building a fresh new life. Life in the UAE was not without its challenges. Such as purchasing a house in a foreign country, finding a suitable school for our daughter, getting used to Middle Eastern bureaucracy as well as cultural norms was another rapid learning curve. However, with each challenge, we met it head-on, overcame and adapted. We were part of a flourishing community and felt like we had found our tribe. It was a beautiful journey that spanned six wonderful years.

The Thorn of Infertility

The pursuit of a sibling for our daughter led to unchartered territory - Infertility. Month after month, year after year, our hopes were dashed with the arrival of my period, leaving behind a flood of tears and a lingering sense of despair. The dream of a growing family was met with unexpected roadblocks. After many years of trying to conceive naturally, we decided to pursue IVF treatment despite its invasive nature, only to uncover a larger obstacle. A tennis ball-sized cyst on one of my ovaries demanded immediate attention.

The relief post-surgery was short-lived, as the biopsy revealed precancerous cells, throwing our world into a whirlwind of fear, confusion, emotions, and uncertainty. A year of consultations with specialists in the UAE and London marked a transformative period. Mindset shifts, nutritional adjustments, and lifestyle changes all contributed to a natural conception. A miracle after the struggles we had been through. Our firstborn son blessed our family in early 2012.

While enjoying our miracle baby and exclusively breastfeeding our son, another pregnancy took us by surprise. For the first few days of the surprise pregnancy, I was worried about how I would manage having a newborn, being pregnant, and having a 6-year-old active daughter with no family support. Yet, this conundrum was also short-lived, as a miscarriage at eight weeks brought a new kind of grief that we had not experienced before.

Losing the foetus proved to us that expanding our family was what we wanted to do, no matter how hard it would be. A few months later, I was pregnant again, and this time, there was no fear or concern about coping or having my hands full. In May 2013, just 17 months apart, we were blessed with our second son. The celebrations were brutally cut short, and our lives changed forever with the sudden death of my mother in front of my eyes due to a massive heart attack. Scenes that forever haunt me and became frequent visitors in my nightmares. Four weeks postpartum, my life felt like it had ended, and I would never be able to overcome this huge loss. I thought that I would never be able to smile again or feel joy again. My heart felt physically shattered, an intensity level that I had never felt before. Navigating the postpartum period in mourning was the saddest chapter of my life; depths of despair and depression took hold, but I suffered in silence, not asking for help or support.

I had to be strong for the sake of our young children, especially for our daughter, who was grieving hard. The ensuing years were marked by depression, grief, despair, therapy, and the gradual process of healing. Despite the tumultuous journey, my resilience and faith allowed me to navigate the challenges and emerge scarred but stronger and wiser.

Navigating Storms: A Journey from sunny UAE to windy Yorkshire

The decision to uproot a well-established life in the vibrant UAE and return to the UK, specifically Yorkshire, in the middle of winter probably wasn't the best idea.

It was a decision not made lightly. The transition from the sunny embrace of the Middle East to the bitterly cold, unpredictable weather of Yorkshire had to be carefully weighed in the balance. My mother's death made us realise that we needed to be close to family once again.

December in Yorkshire is known for its biting cold and relentless storms. This not only posed a challenge in terms of adjusting to a drastically different climate but also ushered in a season of mental and emotional storms. The young, ambitious woman from London who once embraced the cosmopolitan lifestyle in Dubai now found herself in a small rural town. Feeling like a fish completely out of water, gasping to stay alive. Transitioning from a life of relative ease and home help in Dubai to the confines of cramped accommodation in Yorkshire was a stark reality check. Adding to the complexity, our daughter had to navigate the emotional challenges of joining a new school mid-term in a different country. The responsibility to regulate not only my own emotions and resentments but also those of our daughter was a difficult task. The resilience required during this period became the foundation of a new personality that I had to develop. A drastically different personality evolved, vastly contrasting the naive and playful soul that I had been up until then.

My husband, due to work commitments, continued to work abroad while I managed the day-to-day struggles in the UK. Living in cramped accommodation with the in-laws only intensified the pressure. However, it wasn't until months later, after enduring the strains of tight living quarters and other personal challenges, that I decided to move out with our three young kids.

Eventually, life began to ease up, and a semblance of normalcy was restored. I felt like I could finally breathe in my own space, and the journey towards establishing a new life in Yorkshire took a more positive turn.

Wellies, mud, and tiny footprints: Life as a Property Renovator

Living in rented accommodation was not ideal, and an impulse buy at auction catapulted my husband and me into the journey of property renovation. Wellies became a staple, mud a constant companion, and the symphony of contractors and surveyors played as the soundtrack to our days.

The children became regulars onsite, experiencing firsthand the transformation their home was undergoing. Endless trips to merchant yards to get supplies hardened me in ways I could have never imagined. The renovation process was far from smooth sailing due to the complexity and scale of the project. Building challenges emerged like unexpected storms, and the planning department became a battleground. Back-and-forth negotiations, paperwork, and countless hurdles tested our resolve. Amid all the chaos, we persevered, undeterred by the hurdles that arose at every turn.

After nearly twelve months of mud, disagreements, executive decisions, and disputes, our vision materialised into reality. The property, once a dilapidated bungalow, now stood tall as a double-story house. This is a testament to our unwavering determination and passion for transformation. From the depths of rubble emerged a shiny new home, a labour of love that surpassed the challenges and reflected our commitment to creating a home of our own for our family. Finally, we were happy and settled into our new life in Yorkshire with our children and pets. As one challenge ended, another began…

A Teacher's Journey: Balancing Dreams, challenges, and Unforeseen Turns

The desire to become an Early Years teacher sparked within me during my time working as a Teaching Assistant in the UAE. Driven by this desire, I set upon training to become an Early Years Practitioner with the view of eventually training to become a teacher. Little did I know that this path would be marked by not only the triumphs but also the unexpected storms of life.

Balancing work, studies, and raising a young family became a delicate dance, demanding endurance and resilience. The days were long, and the nights of studying made them even longer. This journey became a testament to my determination and endurance as I was aligned with my passion. The joy of working with children fueled me, and I loved my job as every day was different. Seeing the children grow in leaps and bounds gave me great satisfaction and a job with purpose. It seemed that the pieces were falling into place, and the dreams I had envisioned were finally coming true.

In the midst of professional achievement, life threw an unexpected curveball. My brother gave me the shocking news that my father had been diagnosed with stage 4 Cancer. This delivered a blow that reverberated through our entire family. It had only been a few years before that we had lost our mother. The trajectory of my life changed once again, with the weight of concern and the need to be there for my father taking precedence over my professional pursuits.

Endurance became the flavour of my life as I navigated the challenges of my father's health while continuing to fulfil my roles as an early years practitioner, parent, daughter, and sister. Faced with the harsh reality of his diagnosis, our father made a courageous decision to venture down an unconventional path. He focused on optimising nutrition, exploring alternative treatments, and maintaining a positive mindset that defied the looming spectre of death.

Against all odds, our father lived a normal and independent life until just a few months before his eventual passing. The juxtaposition of life and death became an intricate dance, highlighting the power of choice and mindset, even in the face of the inevitable. The commitment to be there for my father necessitated frequent travels between Yorkshire and London, and the desire to spend precious moments with him drove me to overcome my fear of motorway driving.

On the first few trips, I drove with my hands shaking on the steering wheel, crying at service stations, and praying to get to my destination safely. This emotional and physical toll, added to the demands of a week working with energetic children, reached a point where HR intervened. The ultimatum finally came- a choice between family and the job that I loved.

With a heavy heart, I made the decision, once again putting family above career. The moment when HR pulled me aside for a quiet word served as a catalyst, prompting a profound promise to myself. At that moment, I vowed never to work for anyone else again, determined to become my boss regardless of the challenges that lay ahead.

Healing Journeys: From Resignation to Resilience in Alternative Therapy

As I closed the chapter on a career in education, a new theme in my life began to unfold—one rooted in the healing traditions that had been an integral part of my life from childhood. Coming from India, where the roots of Ayurveda run deep, our family carried a profound respect for traditional and natural medicine. Homoeopathic treatments from childhood and herbal remedies nestled in the family cupboard were not just practices; they were ingrained principles of healing that resonated within our cultural heritage.

The decision to retrain in alternative therapy came with its own set of challenges, not the least of which was being surrounded by a younger demographic at college. Enrolling in my late 30s, I embarked on a journey that demanded resilience and a willingness to start from scratch. The college experience, though enlightening, was a unique adventure as I found myself immersed in a sea of 18-20 year olds.

Despite the age difference, my enthusiasm for the course and the subject matter eclipsed any feelings of being out of place. Learning new skills and delving into the intricacies of alternative therapy became a joyous endeavour.

The classroom transformed into a space where my passion could come alive, and I could dream of future possibilities. The culmination of my efforts was marked by a significant achievement—graduating with a Distinction *.

Becoming my own boss: A leap of faith

After reading several books such as 'Feel the Fear and Do It Anyway' by Susan Jeffers, 'Awaken the Giant Within' by Tony Robbins, and others, I was left feeling inspired and courageous. Countless discussions later with my husband and a close friend, we decided to take the financial plunge to open our therapy clinic. This marked a courageous leap into the unknown. Excitement mixed with fear and the bliss of ignorance propelled us forward. The doors opened with trepidation, and in that moment, I became the architect of my professional destiny...... or I thought I had!

The clinic wasn't just a business but an extension of myself, my baby, and my sanctuary. Blood, sweat, and tears were poured into its creation. Juggling the responsibilities of being a mother, a therapist, and a business owner required burning the candle at both ends and a huge learning curve once again. In the chaos and trials, I found purpose, and the clinic became a sanctuary for healing and transformation for both my clients and myself.

Out of the blue, the world was struck by the global pandemic, and the clinic, deemed non-essential and high-risk, faced an eight-month closure. It was a time of uncertainty, a test of resilience. Months of stress and fear compounded, and my mental health suffered. When the doors finally reopened, it felt like a phoenix rising from the ashes. The COVID-19 experience prompted a profound mindset shift in me. Determined not to let external factors dictate my fate once again, I decided to pivot the business into a new direction. With a renewed resilience and a thirst for knowledge, I delved into the world of Hypnotherapy, specifically the Rapid Transformational Therapy (RTT©) method so I could offer remote services as well as in-person services.

I added Energy Healing and Mizan Therapy to my repertoire of therapies that could be done remotely and in person. The metaphysical world opened up, and many paradigm and profound consciousness shifts occurred. Awakenings, as much as we want them to be magical experiences, are often the opposite: a painful shattering and then recalibration.

The journey of retraining as a Hypnotherapist in the RTT© method was intense, marked by the loss of two maternal aunts within a few months of each other. It seemed that grief had become a recurring theme in my life. That year, laced with loss, sheer exhaustion from all the juggling, and grief, culminated in my graduation as a Certified Hypnotherapist and RTT ©Therapist. Tears of joy filled my eyes at achieving this huge milestone. Standing on stage with my mentor, Marisa Peer, was surreal and a moment I will cherish forever.

The Cost of Success: Navigating the Slow Descent into Burn-out

The journey towards burn-out is often a subtle and silent one, a winding road that winds its way into one's life without warning. The pursuit of success in various roles - as a mother, wife, daughter-in-law, businesswoman, therapist, and eternal student, led down a path where the price of accomplishment turned out to be the slow erosion of personal, physical, and mental well-being.

In the relentless pursuit of success, I became a master juggler, adept at balancing all the various demands placed upon me. Hyper-focused on achieving excellence in each role, I proudly wore the title of being 'crazy busy' as a badge of honour, proud of my ability to manage a multitude of responsibilities simultaneously. Yet, beneath the surface, the silent descent into burn-out was underway. Ignoring the subtle warnings, the signs of exhaustion, irritability, insomnia, IBS, and sudden bouts of anxiety all became uninvited guests.

The relentless pace of a hectic life was taking a toll, gradually sapping away the energy reserves that once fueled me. The energy and enthusiasm that once fueled my achievements were now depleted, and the invisible toll on both physical and mental well-being manifested itself.

In a sudden moment, the reality of burn-out hit with the force of impact, stopping me in my tracks and making me bed-bound for weeks. The relentless pace that had defined my life for the last decade came to a screeching halt. The very success that had been the goal became the source of a profound and unexpected crisis. Weeks in bed forced me to reflect and rethink what was important and where I was headed.

Around the same time, a routine blood test showed that I had become dangerously close to pre-diabetes, my triglycerides were too high, I had elevated cholesterol, and my blood pressure was also elevated. The 'Deadly Quadrant' had struck me. As someone with PCOS and insulin resistance, my bloodwork was not a shock to my GP. However, for me, it was a huge wake-up call. My weight over the years had slowly crept up as I was eating on the go due to my busy schedule as well as stress eating. Things had to change, otherwise I would end up with the same fate as my late mother, and this scared the living daylights out of me.

The pursuit of excellence had come at the cost of personal health, and the journey toward balance began - a recalibration of priorities, a redefinition of success, and a commitment to self-care and fitness. Despite having had a personal trainer for the previous two years and working out weekly with him, I still developed all these conditions. I knew that unless I addressed my diet and particularly my chronic stress, things would progress in a direction of accelerated disease.

The Bittersweet Farewell: Closing the Clinic, Letting Go, and Prioritising Health

The decision to close this chapter of my life was not just about letting go of a business; it was about confronting the question:

Was it truly time to release something that had become so intertwined with my identity and ambition for the sake of my health and family? The badge of honour became a weight that needed to be shed. Quite literally!

The clinic had been more than just a professional space; it had served as a sanctuary during times of personal struggle. It was a place of healing, not only for my clients but also for myself. The thought of closing its doors meant bidding farewell to a refuge that had played a pivotal role in my journey out of depression and grief.

Health and family emerged as the ultimate priorities. The clinic, despite all its significance, became a chapter that needed to close for the sake of a healthier, more balanced life. It was a profound choice, acknowledging that success and identity should not come at the expense of well-being and familial bonds.

Metamorphosis: Confronting identity, redefining success, and embracing self-compassion

Closing the clinic felt like a seismic shift in my life, challenging preconceptions about identity, purpose, success, and failure. The closure, initially perceived as a personal failure, became a catalyst for transformation. Seeking professional help from a life coach, I navigated self-identity, what success meant to me, loss, and purpose. Through the guidance of my life coach, I was able to reframe and grow. Shadow work and inner child work with an RTT© colleague helped me identify crucial links and forced me to ask myself difficult questions about identity. Stripped of the professional label, I grappled with the question of who I was without the clinic.

My life coach, Fatima Rasool, a beacon of wisdom, guided me to view failure not as a verdict but as a teacher. It became an opportunity for compassion towards myself and a catalyst for personal and professional growth, albeit in a different direction. Swallowing the bitter pill of change was an initial challenge, but it paved the way for metamorphosis. The closure, reframed by Fatima, became a stepping stone towards a more authentic, compassionate, and personally defined version of success.

As the clinic doors closed, tears flowed freely. Each drop was a testament to the countless healing journeys, the lives touched, and the gratitude for those who had entrusted me with their healing and well-being. In that moment of closure, there was a deep acknowledgement of the impact made and the significance of the healing space. The decision to let go was not a surrender but a conscious choice rooted in faith and a profound belief that greater things lay ahead.

A deep-seated faith became the guiding force in my life. The belief that God had intricate plans, woven with purpose and promise, offered solace. In the quiet aftermath of closure, there was an unwavering commitment to keep the faith and allow life's currents to guide the way. Going with the flow became my mantra, acknowledging that rigidity might obscure future opportunities and blessings that await in the unexpected turns of the river of life.

My new mindset was 'without health, there was nothing'. The pursuit of true wealth transcended material success, aligning with the richness found in physical and mental health. If I had my health and my family, I had everything. Without health and loved ones, life loses its essence and joy.

Embracing Slow Living: A Year of Transition, Reflection, and Renewed Foundations

The eight months of professional hibernation became a pivotal period in my life—an intentional pause that allowed a shift from the fast-paced, high-achiever mentality to a more nurturing and reflective state. This transformative year was not only about personal rejuvenation but also about going back to the basics. My focus shifted consciously toward my family.

With our eldest child applying for university to study Veterinary Medicine, our eldest son transitioning to secondary school, and our youngest son in the final year of primary school, the importance of maternal presence became paramount.

Guiding and supporting our children through significant milestones and offering reassurance and care during a period of considerable change brought immense peace and contentment to my being.

Shifting Energies: From Masculine to Feminine

The hiatus allowed a shift from the masculine energy that I had adopted for the last decade. The energy of hustling, of hyper ambition, independence, and achievement. I realised that I had lost my softness, and now it was time to find my feminine energy of receiving and nurturing once again. Slow living replaced the decades of fast-paced living. Fast food was replaced with slow-cooked, homemade nourishing food. Rushed conversations were replaced with intentional listening.

This pause offered an opportunity to savour precious moments, appreciate the present, and engage in the art of nurturing oneself and the family. I got used to saying "No" to social gatherings, and FOMO was replaced with peace. Once again, I picked up the paintbrush and my tool kit to create a sanctuary in our home so family time could be prioritised. Despite the clinic being closed, I was still getting desperate requests for appointments and people in crisis. My heart felt guilty as my nature is to always help, especially if I have been asked directly for help. Saying "No" to loyal clients was a painful process, but I had to for the sake of my health and family- both of which had been neglected for far too long.

Once again, I turned to RTT© and life coaching to help me with my boundary issues, in particular the difficulty I had saying "No" to people. Finding the root cause of this issue was enlightening and made saying "No" much easier, and the associated feelings of guilt reduced significantly. This mindset shift saved me from many hours of guilt and feeling like I was a bad person. The gift of time is a beautiful one, and it opened a space for contemplation. I reflected on the profound questions about life's meaning, the legacy that I desired to leave behind, and the vision for the second half of my life. It was a journey of self-discovery and intentional living.

The professional hibernation allowed my husband and I to embark on a second honeymoon, a celebration of 21 years of marriage. We were able to reflect on life's ups and downs, the adversities we had faced, and the resilience that fortified our bond. The foundations of love were not only revisited but renewed. A newfound respect developed between us, and a calm place of serene understanding grew. With this new dynamic, our conflicts and resentments lessened, leading to a more harmonious partnership, one that positively impacted the ambience at home.

Joining a Like-Minded Team: Allies in the Journey

When you set a clear intention, God, the Universe, a higher power, or your mind, whatever you believe in, makes it happen. I had been diagnosed with bursitis and tendonitis in my shoulders due to overexertion and had been attending physiotherapy sessions for the previous six months.

Despite all of those sessions and being on painkillers, my pain was still present. Once again, I turned to alternative therapies and started acupuncture sessions with Amanda Crawshaw, a wonderful acupuncturist whom I had seen previously for other issues. As the sessions progressed, I told my story of burn-out and ill-health, followed by a period of professional hiatus to recover. Our weekly sessions provided me with an empathetic ear with a person with whom I felt professionally and personally aligned. We had similar life experiences and bonded quickly.

One thing I had missed having my own business was colleagues. The life of a solo-entrepreneur can be very lonely. When the opportunity of sharing the clinic with Amanda one or two days a week came up I jumped at the opportunity. Working part-time in an established and respected clinic was exactly what I had been praying for.

I am once again in a good space, feeling excited to work alongside some fantastic practitioners, experts in their fields, and passionate about what they offer.

Our collective mindset is perfectly aligned, sharing common values and goals. The future now is one of renewed energy, passion, courage, and the exhilarating journey into the unknown, all with a harmonious balance and the ability to stop and say "No". A sentence that I had struggled with since my childhood.

The future promises a departure from societal expectations of success. I am ready to define success on my terms, creating a narrative that aligns with my personal values, aspirations, faith, and a vision that is my own.

If you have felt inspired by my journey, then please do give me a follow on my social media or leave a comment. If you would like to work with me, please contact me via my linktree or email address.

Email: info.saffrontherapies@gmail.com
Website: www.saffrontherapies.com
Instagram: www.instagram.com/saffron.therapies
Linktr.ee: www.linktr.ee/aishabeg

> *"Define success on your terms, because there is only one you and only one life to live, be the master of your destiny by mastering your mindset!"* Aisha Beg

CHAPTER 10
Suzanne Robinson

Writer, storyteller, and content creator

From Silent Struggle to Shared Strength
The Long-awaited Appointment

I remember the day I finally went to see the dermatologist. I felt a rollercoaster of emotions – anxious because hospitals weren't my favourite place and apprehensive about what seeing a dermatologist could lead to. It felt like a big jump from being treated by my GP at the local surgery to needing to be referred to a specialist. My GP, who was supportive, had tried every steroid cream and emollient ointment they could think of to help me, but it just kept getting worse. I also felt a little relieved and hopeful that although the past few years had been difficult and my psoriasis was so very sore, I had to have faith that I would receive the support and treatment I so desperately needed, so that I could go on to live my life without psoriasis calling the shots.

I sat in the waiting room at the hospital with my notebook in hand, ready to explain why I needed treatment. You see, like so many others, I had done my research. I had been living with this autoimmune disease without a day's respite for many years, and it wasn't getting any easier. I was ready for a battle if a battle was required! Why was I ready for a battle? My emotions were all over the place. I felt nervous because I did not know what to expect, and I was on my own. One thing was for certain. I was determined I wouldn't leave the hospital without a treatment plan. I had to make sure that I made the most of this appointment with the dermatologist so that I could secure a positive outcome.

My name was called, and I walked into the room. I sat down, and before I could say anything, the tears came flooding out. I was sobbing harder than I ever had before, and it took me by surprise because I wasn't expecting to react like that at all. Looking back, I now know why I reacted the way I did. I had waited for this appointment for so long, about three years, give or take a couple of months. A lot was riding on this. My body had changed so much; my confidence was at an all-time low, and I felt hopeless and very alone. I was hoping for help, support, and reassurance. I needed to know that there was light at the end of this very long tunnel because I couldn't see it for myself. Thankfully, the dermatologist I saw that day was very kind and patient with me. She doesn't know this and probably never will, but that day, I felt as though she was my guardian angel. She could have hurried me along but instead took the time to listen to my worries and concerns. She really listened to how I felt and showed compassion and understanding. She waited for me to calm down, examined me and reassured me that all she wanted to do was to help. After she left the room for a few minutes, I hastily fixed the eyeliner that was running down my face, sat up straight, and restored my composure. When she returned, with an appointment card in her hand, she explained that I should come back the very next day for an assessment and then my first course of treatment would begin. The sense of relief I felt was immense and rather overwhelming.

A Glimpse of Happiness

Leaving the hospital that day, I felt happier and more relieved than I had in years. I had the biggest smile on my face, a spring in my step, and a feeling of hope in my heart (for the first time in a very long time). I had taken a huge step in the right direction. Even though I was apprehensive beforehand, and I had no idea what to expect. The outcome was more than I dared hope for. As I hopped, skipped, and jumped onto the bus home, I was still smiling. I had no idea what the other passengers must have thought. There I was, sitting on my own, smiling like a Cheshire cat. I couldn't have cared, to be honest. I felt happy, really happy. I liked feeling this way, an overwhelming sense of hope washed over me. Hope that I had been heard. Hope that I was going to get the treatment I needed and hope that the future was going to be brighter and happier. The reason these feelings meant so much to me at that time was because I had the sudden realisation that I had been feeling hopeless for far too long. Hopefulness to me feels like a superpower because what do we have without hope? I loved this feeling, and I wanted to feel this way more of the time. In fact, this whole experience reminded me just how sad I had become.

To describe it in more detail, I related it to Christmas morning as a child or my wedding day. You know that feeling in your tummy, I call it butterflies. That feeling of nervous excitement. I was about to embark on a new treatment plan. The treatment wasn't new, but it was new to me. I had every faith in the medical team taking care of me and the treatment being offered. I wanted to bottle up these happy emotions and share them with anyone who needed them.

This is when the seed was planted. I shifted my focus from feeling overwhelmed and sorry for myself, to wanting to find ways to take care of my emotional wellbeing so that I could create a space for positivity in my life. Thinking about how I felt in that moment, I realised there had to be a way for me to feel like this more often. It hit me that true happiness had been missing from my life for far too long. It dawned on me that the sad moments far outweighed the happy ones, and I had to do something about it. When faced with the choice between hope or hopelessness, hope won every time. There wasn't a choice to make if I was going to learn how to live with this skin condition in a more positive way, some pretty significant changes had to be made. I made the decision to embrace change and to make a conscious effort to look for the good in my life every day.

This realisation led me to commit to a journey of self-discovery and emotional transformation. I dug deep into my feelings. As I dismantled the barriers I had built up, I replaced them with a newfound commitment to find the joy in my life. The truth is happiness wasn't the destination; instead, it's an ongoing journey, one that continues to take effort alongside the decision every day to work on my emotional well-being. I also acknowledged that choosing hope wasn't about denying the challenges I faced. Instead, it was about facing them head on and finding ways to live with them instead of making them my main focus in life. Whilst on this journey, I understood that chasing happiness was a deliberate and courageous choice I made.

The Journey to Self-Care and Sharing my Story

The saying that 'life is a journey' is so true. We are all on this earth to learn from the happy times as well as the challenges we encounter. In fact, I believe that we learn so much more from the difficulties we face. I also think that we inevitably change over time. Everything I have experienced since childhood, right through to the present day, has moulded me into the person I am today. We become a source of valuable knowledge and information. How we use this to influence our lives in a positive way is what matters most.

We all carry thoughts and emotions from our past with us. Although our experiences might be similar, our individual responses and the emotions linked to them are unique to each of us. How do we handle this baggage? Personally, I view it like maintaining a mental filing cabinet. I file away everything I have learnt along the way. Allowing myself to release any unnecessary weight whilst ensuring I don't repeat the same mistake twice. All of the essential knowledge and useful skills I have learnt are stored at the front for easy access for when I need them. It is all about managing what stays with us, like a well-organised mental archive. Learning to embrace life with a visible skin condition and pursuing self-acceptance has been a gradual process, requiring patience and a slow-burning positivity.

I dedicated time each day to focus on self-care, highlighting everything in my life that I felt grateful for. At the start, I did this by writing down ten things every morning in my gratitude journal. I also mapped out a morning routine that became non-negotiable. Activities such as taking a walk, journaling, meditating and listening to a podcast to learn something new or music that I found uplifting. Whatever it was, I made sure it was something I could engage in, after all, I was investing my time, and this intentional effort led to a positive shift in my mindset. I discovered that by focusing on self-improvement and learning to appreciate all of the blessings in my life, I rediscovered self-love. Psoriasis stopped being the focus of my day, and I started to talk openly about living with this visible skin condition. By this point in my life, I had been living with 'p', as I like to call it, for six years. I know it must sound very strange when I say that apart from the medical team looking after me, only a handful of people in my life knew I had psoriasis. It saddens me to say now but at the time due to feeling embarrassed I had kept it a secret. Looking back, I know that doing this weighed heavy on my heart and, I'm sure, didn't help the situation at all. Once I had learnt to accept that psoriasis was a part of me, my perspective became more optimistic, and those around me noticed a positive change in me.

I decided to prioritise happiness, remembering the day I saw the dermatologist, and reliving the genuine joy I felt. Living with psoriasis for over a decade now and openly discussing it in recent years has supported me through some pretty dark times, especially during the psoriasis flares I have experienced over the years.

Through openly expressing the emotional impact of psoriasis and recognising the loneliness I experienced before confiding in family, close friends, other patients, and the medical professionals, I had a revelation. I definitely wasn't alone. There were others out there who were facing challenges similar to mine. I decided to share my story. I know, it's a bold move. I went from pretty much keeping it to myself to posting my story on my social media platforms, hoping to connect with those who could relate to my experiences living with psoriasis. The thought of anyone else feeling as unhappy as I did was the driving force behind making this decision.

Finding a Passion for Writing

Through this transformation, I've embarked on a journey of self-discovery and personal growth, channelling my passion for writing whilst sharing my story about living with psoriasis. Although the path was winding, the highs and the lows led the way to a renewed sense of purpose and a commitment to embrace my true self. For far too long, I hesitated and held myself back by concerns about others' opinions. The fear of judgement kept me from fully expressing myself. Through the art of writing, I opened up about my often-turbulent journey with 'p', choosing words over images and delving into the depth of my experiences. I had no idea when I started putting pen to paper just how freeing this process would be. This shift wasn't easy. It required me to prioritise my own well-being. Yet, as I redirected my focus, my social circle expanded. This is when my group 'Storytellers of Purpose' was created. Forming a community, I am immensely proud of. Saying 'yes' to daunting challenges became my mantra, which led to impactful moments where my words resonated with others, inspiring them on their own journeys.

One of the most gratifying experiences is receiving messages from my readers and group members, expressing how the content I share has inspired them to share their stories too. These interactions continue to fuel my commitment to support others through the words I write and the writing tips I share with my group members, whether that's in a group setting or on a 1-1 basis.

I have come to realise that acceptance, love and kindness are the foundations of genuine connections. I choose to share my story through the written word, ensuring that authenticity is what drives me. I am grateful for the journey, from not knowing how sharing my story would be received but doing it anyway because it felt like the right thing to do, to supporting others to do the same. With the support of my mentors and the incredible community we have created, I have not only rediscovered my passion for writing, but I have also taken the initiative to create a space for other storytellers and content creators to do the same.

Anticipating the future brings exciting possibilities as my dedication to storytelling evolves. I plan to use my platform to encourage others to share their stories, fostering a community where shared experiences become a source of support. Collaborative projects are underway, including my own book chronicling a decade of living with psoriasis. As I embark on this new chapter, I aim to strengthen existing connections and cultivate new ones. The potential of storytelling is boundless, and I firmly believe that everyone has a story to tell. My goal is to contribute to a world where authenticity is celebrated, and our stories resonate far and wide.

Thriving Through Purposeful Storytelling

I am stepping into this next part of my journey with the word 'THRIVE'. The challenges I have faced, particularly living with psoriasis for many years, have become the stepping stones towards both my personal and professional growth.

Accepting the changes psoriasis has brought into my life has been a tough process and, at times, a pretty bumpy road to travel. Through self-care and embracing self-love, I have grown to 'love the skin I'm in'. Not everyone stuck around to see this transformation, and that's okay. Some people grow with you, and others don't. Letting go of those who couldn't accept this new me paved the way for incredible changes. I am grateful for the new connections and opportunities that have come into my life.

Whether I am sharing my story, raising awareness, supporting my group members, or diving into the art of content creation, each experience has led to many positive outcomes. These include – personal development, connections with like-minded individuals, and the creation of a supportive community. This journey is just beginning, with exciting projects ready to unfold. It's not just about personal success; it's about us thriving together. The goal is to nurture a passion for storytelling.

While we all continue to manoeuvre our way through this life, dealing with the challenges we face, I know that life has taught me how important it is to seek out and to give support. Together, we can build communities whereby we celebrate our achievements while supporting each other through the challenging times.

We journey through life side by side, encountering shared triumphs and tribulations. However, our perceptions vary, influenced by our distinct perspectives and emotional responses. As time passes, feelings towards specific moments may fade. By documenting these experiences in real time, we create a tangible record. Reading these notes in the future becomes a metaphorical journey back in time, allowing us to relive the essence of these moments.

Be genuine, stay true to who you are, and let your story resonate with the people meant to be a part of your journey.

Linktree: @suzannerobinsonstoryteller

CHAPTER 11

Jacky Allan

Owner at Jacky O Allan, Coach, Author and Digital Marketer

An Entrepreneur Daring to Dream

A little bit about my story...

For as long as I can remember, my life has been weighed down with responsibility; I have always taken care of something or someone else, as helping others is what I love to do, and now I believe it is my purpose in life.

I left school with minimal qualifications, dabbled in a corporate city job for a few months, and then found myself as assistant manager at a country house hotel, where I used to be a part-time waitress through school. After a year out of education and in the working world, I returned to education and went to university to fulfil my dream of becoming a paediatric nurse, which didn't play out as expected because of internal struggles arising in my life at that time.

Leaving University after one year led me back to the working world where I got a job as a trainee car salesperson at one of the biggest dealerships in the city (at that time). This is where I started to see the value of money, and every maths lesson suddenly fell into place. So if I learn this, sell that, then I'll receive ££££. I quickly learned and understood this system, and it was something that no one in my world had ever done before. I was the first to be a Uni dropout.

A serious relationship then evolved from working in this job, and at the young age of nineteen, I was love-struck. The relationship progressed pretty quickly and before I knew it, I left everything and everyone I knew behind, packed my life into one suitcase and emigrated to Australia to start a new life. I was petrified and excited; it was a huge move at twenty-two years of age, and the experience did not start smoothly. On night one the house we were renting got broken into and we lost everything. Worse than that they broke in when we were upstairs sleeping, and from that moment on I struggled to feel safe and discovered that I was a natural worrier and an overthinker. We found strength to carry on, moved to another part of Australia, got jobs and started building our new life.

By twenty-four, I was in a leadership position in the mining industry and pregnant with my first child, that's when the real responsibility set in, and for me at that time, very quickly it became about how many hats I had to wear and whoever was shouting the loudest got my attention, all whilst being on my own ninety percent of the time. This was the moment that my needs and wants went on the back burner.

I had fallen into the trap of trying to "do all the things" working full time, parenting, keeping house, nurturing my relationship, navigating new friendships and generally being the glue that held everything together.

As time passed, my responsibilities increased, life plans and financial demands soared, my family unit grew to two children, we welcomed a new puppy, and my career took off, which was all exciting and fulfilling, equally extremely demanding, and my identity was lost. It's no wonder that women become so lost and confused while journeying through life that they end up on the hamster wheel until they eventually fall off whilst reaching burnout. I was falling off, reaching burnout but not recognising the signs until they showed up medically as I was diagnosed with an extremely rare eye disease, which forced our family to relocate and return back home to Scotland – to family.

By default, I had landed here in this life, feeling like a failure, living in a state of fear; I felt so lost, scared, lonely and inadequate. I internalised all my fears because from the outside in, I had it all but from the inside out, it couldn't have been further from the truth, and I was using all my strength to put one foot in front of the other as I just could not see a way out.

When you are left to question your whole existence, that's when something HAS to change…

Here I was listening and supporting everybody else's woes while silently questioning mine every single day. Something had to change, and it no longer became about the country I was living in. I was in the unknown, left behind all I knew as an adult and felt like I had taken five steps back in life and had lost all control. I had promised myself that things would change once we moved home and that I would take the time for my young children and be the stay-at-home parent that I always wanted to be. It felt great to have that time and not have to send my youngest to daycare for ten hours a day whilst being at work, but with that came financial paralysis. For the first time in my life, since the age of twelve, I wasn't earning my own money.

I was raising two children, which was a true gift, that I was able to be fully present for them, but all I felt I had really done was replace money for time. I still wasn't any further ahead, and I had just changed out one commodity for another. I was now completely stuck!

I didn't want to have to get a job back in the corporate world, which would lead back to outsourcing childcare again, and equally, I was climbing the walls being a stay-at-home Mum and financially restrained.

There's got to be something that ticks all the boxes…

Surely, in this day and age, women shouldn't have to choose between being a mother and having a career. I couldn't be the only person in the world feeling like this, and deep down, I knew there had to be a solution to my problem.

In the many, many sleepless nights tossing and turning in the middle of the night, trying to think of a solution, I fell victim to the midnight scroll. I would scroll Facebook for hours, observing everybody else's "idyllic" lives, worrying about what I was doing so wrong because my life didn't look like that.

Now, as the social media platforms have evolved, we now know that what we see on people's timelines are only the highlights and that they can be masking the "real life stuff" that is actually going on in their lives, and I feel everyone should remember this when falling into the aimless scrolling trap, but back in 2018 when my world was not how I knew it, I fell head first in the comparison bubble.

Ninety-nine percent of the content I was consuming was the happy family snaps, the negative nancies' point of view and who had what for dinner that night, but then… I came across the one percent, a woman who I had known from a previous low ticket network marketing company (yes, I tried that too) who was on this journey back to self, whilst being a full-time parent AND building a sustainable online business.

My mind was blown; I had never seen anything of the sort. How is this even real? How is she making money online while taking pictures of herself drinking coffee on the beach and still able to do the school pick-up every day? I was utterly confused on how this worked but, at the same time, I believed it was all true. This was the answer, and this is what I had been looking for.

I followed her journey (every day) for eighteen months, and after the bricks-and-mortar business we had invested in fell through, I decided to dive right in and booked the call to find out how I could also create that life for me and my family.

I was so excited about the opportunity and the ability to support others in changing their lives and to be able to change mine at the same time. This was it; the next chapter and I was here for it. Three months into my shiny new business, which had totally cracked me open like an egg, we lost a family member to suicide, which naturally left the family in complete shock and devastation. Six months after that, the world shut down, and suddenly, we were all facing the unknown. Twenty months later my seventeen-year relationship came to an end, and I became a solo parent. These were extremely excruciating times. Life was showing me that things change, they change fast, and I couldn't keep up.

The one thing that kept me going during these times was my online business because it had opened me up to the concept of mindset, something I didn't even know existed until I was thirty-four; it was the only light at the end of a very dark tunnel that I could see.

Finding my way back to self...

I was now in the position where the plan had changed, and everything I thought to be true in my adult life was no longer my truth. I had completely hit rock bottom, and I now had to rebuild myself and my children's lives from the ground up.

This all started with mindset, not in drastic measures either, I baby-stepped into the world of positive thinking, holding onto the belief that this moment in time would pass and that the only way was up. I found gratitude journals and placed daily affirmations all around my house.

To start with, I was like a bull in a China shop and expected everything to get better and move forward overnight. I was doing all the things, but I didn't feel any better. I had to learn how to be. You have to take the time to heal and listen to your body and emotions because, maybe for the first time in your life, you are allowing years and years of trauma and deeply buried emotions to rise to the surface. Accept what is showing up through you today, gently move through the emotion and release it. This is the starting point of rebuilding yourself, and I can assure you that you are not going to stay here forever, as long as you make the choice to take a chance to change your life.

Journal your thoughts daily, get it out of your head onto paper. Release everything that no longer serves you, and with that, you will make space for the things that you actually do want in your life.

As you take these baby steps through your next chapter, you build strength and belief within yourself, as you gradually release your old identity and all the labels previously attached to you, you uncover what truly matters to you and will establish YOUR VALUES.

Before I was at that point of strength and self-belief, I leant into my online community and borrowed their belief in me until I was strong enough to believe in myself. From that and as I started to see my worth again, I began to invest in myself. I invested in coaching programs, business-building courses and healing strategies. I re-evaluated my inner circle and cut out all the noise and distractions that no longer served me or that I identified with. When you're going through trauma, everybody seems to want a piece of the action, sometimes with the best intentions and sometimes not.

Please remember that you get to decide who deserves a seat at your table, and not everyone needs to be a part of your story. "You can't heal in the same environment that broke you."

Doors of opportunity began to open…

Your children are a direct reflection of you. They are watching you and modelling their own reactions and emotions from yours. As I began to heal, so did they, as I began to find myself, so did they, and as I began to move forward, so did they. It has been the most rewarding experience as a parent, witnessing the transformation of my children and together creating our new family unit that now feels safe.

Everything that has happened for me to get me to and through these life lessons with precious cargo on board has moulded me into a kinder, calmer, more resilient person and with that my energy has completely changed, and no matter where I go, I will always choose to add value to the spaces and lives around me.

Which comes back to my belief that my purpose in life wasn't to be a medical nurse in a hospital environment, it is to guide, nurture and support other women to be able to step off the hamster wheel of survival, before reaching burnout and be able to create their ideal lifestyle by choosing to do what lights them up every day and never having to sacrifice time for money. To know they are worth more and that they can be an amazing mother to their children and excel in a thriving business that creates a legacy for said children. It doesn't have to be one or the other. I believe that everyone should be given the same opportunity in life regardless of their background, labels or academic achievements. An abundant life is available to us all; we just have to say yes to ourselves. Saying yes to the unknown and taking risks has led me to once-in-a-lifetime opportunities like flying out to Florida, USA and being interviewed on Fox TV, writing my story right here for others to be able to pull inspiration from and know that they can achieve all of this too.

This is only the beginning of my entrepreneurial journey. I'm navigating my way through my coaching qualification alongside my online business, and nothing excites me more than to be financially independent, living my truth, and creating an impact with a complete life of choice.

Changing my narrative and being able to re-write my story all started with someone within my inner circle granting me a permission slip, reminding me that I deserved happiness too, and at that time of being scared, lonely, lost and numb, this was the exact reminder that I needed.

So, I am here to remind you that the power to rewrite your story lies within you. You have the permission to create an incredible new identity that aligns with the person you truly are. Trust your intuition, stay focused and enjoy the transformative process.

You are capable of achieving great things; you are more than the label that someone else has given you. You are a woman with dreams, talents and ambitions and I am here to support you and cheer you on as we navigate through this journey together.

Jacky x

Jacky Allan

Life & Business Coach Digital Entrepreneur

Facebook: www.facebook.com/JackyOAllan
Instagram: Jacky Allan (@jackyoallan)
Linktree: www.linktr.ee/jackyallan

CHAPTER 12

Michelle Wynne

Digital Creator/Author

Embracing Self-Worth: A Journey from Imposter Syndrome to Self-Belief and everything in-between

Self-doubt and the echoing voices of imposter syndrome

For as long as I can remember, I have battled with self-doubt and the echoing voices of imposter syndrome, but I learnt to mask it very well.

I appeared confident when communicating and working with people, but I always felt nervous about embarrassing myself, saying the wrong thing, etc. I was never good enough, clever enough, or knowledgeable enough in any situation, as far as I was concerned.

From a very young age, all I wanted to do was work for myself in some creative form. But I never, ever thought that it would actually happen. I'm not confident enough, not clever enough, jack of all trades, master of none, the self-doubt went on and on. The idea of trying to work for myself and failing just fuelled the self-doubt even more. The imposter syndrome clung tightly, often obscuring my true potential. I found myself in a relentless battle against the lingering whispers of inadequacy that swirled around in the recesses of my mind. I always believed that my accomplishments were a mere stroke of luck! Each achievement seemed to be accompanied by an unrelenting voice casting doubt on my abilities.

Where it all began

I grew up in the north of England with my parents and two brothers. It was a happy childhood, and I enjoyed school with wonderful friends. I have great memories. But I wasn't very academic, I did okay, I always just got by. Apart from art, which I loved, I knew I would like to work in a creative space one day. My mind was made up, and I decided to study art. I passed my end-of-school exams, just enough to apply for an Art foundation course, and to my relief, I got in. I was very excited and looking forward to this new life, now I could shine, be more confident, believe in myself, and maybe excel in something.

I enjoyed the course, met lots of new friends, and enjoyed all the various forms of art we investigated and learnt about; time went quickly, and before I knew it, it was the end of the course, and luckily (yes, luck!) I passed.

Now, the decision time came to choose what field to study that would turn into a potential career. But I just couldn't decide; again, I didn't know where my best skills lay; I didn't think I excelled in any area. So, I went with the majority of the group and went down the graphic design route.

Let's go back to 1988, when technology was almost nonexistent. We did not study on computers back then Macs didn't exist, and all our work was geared around your creative abilities, on paper! I really enjoyed the course and loved coming up with various pieces of art related to the tasks, but it was quite obvious (in my head) that everyone was better than me. Again, I never felt like I had the right skills, ideas, etc. Everyone's work was way superior to mine! My daily thoughts. I was always embarrassed to showcase and present my work, even though I never got any bad comments; I just got good advice. My anxiety, embarrassment, and self-doubt constantly chipped away at me.

Fast forward a year, and my home life was taking a turn for the worse. After a turbulent few years, my parents separated, which was not a great surprise, if I'm honest. But it hit me harder than I thought it would, and let's just say studying and coursework took a back seat while I enjoyed Uni life to the fullest.

Looking back, it was as if I'd been given an excuse to fail. I'd feared I would fail anyway, so I gave it a helping hand. I just constantly felt I was not good enough to make it. Well, the inevitable happened, and, wait for it, yes, you guessed it, I failed. When I explained my situation to the tutors, they very kindly gave me a year to pull it back. I think this was the first time I felt true gratitude about anything. had to resubmit my work the next year. I really had to dig deep to complete this, but I did, and I finally graduated a year later than I should have (with help from a very good friend guiding me! Again, I was truly grateful). I did not excel, but I passed all the same. I didn't even go for the graduation ceremony or photo, I felt embarrassed it had taken another year for me to graduate. Because of my self-doubt, I don't have a memory of this achievement in my life, and I know now it truly was an achievement.

It was time to step up and get a job. Did I start to apply for jobs in the graphic design industry? No, of course not; I only just passed, not good enough, and didn't have the computer skills needed, as technological advances had progressed and I was a year behind everyone! I felt at a loss. My thoughts were, where do I go from here? But I knew I had to get out there and earn some money. I had no choice.

Let's continue for the next ten years!

So, to say I was a bit of a lost soul at first was an understatement. I needed the money; I needed to work; that was the focus.

Here goes… I picked up the local paper and scanned for any job vacancies. And my working life began. I went from being a part-time shoe shop assistant to the manager after only three months working there. Did I like it? Let's just say I loved shoes and still do; who doesn't, right? Did I like selling them? Hell no! I wondered if this was going to be my life. No, but if working in retail was not for me, what was? I continued for a while, and in my personal life, I met my now hubby. We decided to move in together and search for a house to buy. Which we did, in a beautiful village. We loved it. I was still unhappy at work. But loved my partner and the place we had chosen to call home. Now, let's fast forward… My next endeavour was an embroidery tape puncher, so how did I go from retail to this?

Well, I met an old Uni friend who lived near where my partner (now hubby) and I had bought our home. We chatted, and she was a designer because she believed in herself and was doing well. She said the guy who was the digital designer inputted (tape puncher) was leaving, and they needed someone to be trained and take over. As you can probably imagine, at first, I thought, I can't apply, I have no skills on a computer; I won't be able to do this, etc. But my hubby, as always said, just go for it; you have nothing to lose. And, of course, he was right. I sent my CV in, got an interview, and got the job, all through stress and nervous anxiety.

Did I believe I had done well? No, I thought they were probably desperate; I couldn't find anyone else, blah, blah, blah. It was not what I'd expected, quite boring if I'm honest, but nice people and I continued this for several years, just plodding on and on, what else would I do!

Then, one evening, while out and about, we met a couple who had just moved to the village where we lived. A few months down the line, we became good friends. They both worked in different aspects of advertising. And I loved hearing about what they'd been up to in the workplace. After finding out my qualifications and what I was doing now, they could not believe I had not used my qualifications and knowledge to go into the advertising industry. They saw the potential in me and believed I could do it; I, on the other hand, did not. Anxiety, nerves, you name it, all I could do was just continue doing what I was doing. I didn't want or think I could step outside of my comfort zone. They persevered and continued to talk about how I would smash it, but I just laughed it off, feeling gutted inside.

My hubby told me time and time again to go for it. But I feared if I quit my job and this didn't work, I would have ruined everything. One day, they turned up and gave me some details of an agency looking to employ a production executive; I thought they were crazy; I didn't even know what that was! But they kept on bombarding me to get me to apply. I was so nervous, but I updated my CV, got it sent off, and, to my surprise, I got an interview. As I've done on previous occasions, I masked how I felt and went to the interview. Well, to my surprise and excitement, I got the job; they believed I could do it.

The start of my self-belief journey

Did I believe I'd achieved it myself? No, it was pure luck and help from a friend, which I was truly grateful for, but I hadn't achieved anything; plus, I was scared and anxious to learn now what it was I had to do.

But after six months, I was in full flow and loved it. This was the start of my advertising career. I moved from agency to agency, earning more money each time. I then got headhunted and told them I could drive, and I couldn't. I had to sort this out and did; I took a week off work, booked myself a driving course and lessons every day for 4 hours, and then passed my test on a Friday. I was a nervous wreck every day. I still don't know how I actually did it. But I did. Again, I was more and more confident by the day.

Jump another few years down the line, and I was a successful Project Manager for nearly ten years in various advertising agencies. I loved the work and the social side, and I started to love myself and be proud of myself and my achievements.

I had got to where I wanted to be, with a great agency, fantastic colleagues and friends, and most important to me then, was a great salary. But I started to reflect, I still felt something was missing! Was this the job for life? I was around creative people, which I loved but wasn't using my creative skills. Life went on, and I continued to enjoy working in the advertising industry, but I still longed for a creative space, I believed it would never be my dream job to work for myself in a creative capacity.

The next chapter...

After lots of discussions, pros and cons, we quit our jobs, and we headed off to the sun to start a new life and to live the dream! To say we had a bumpy start is an understatement. We had organised for my husband to work with a family member, which was great until we got ourselves sorted. But unfortunately, he suddenly passed away within two weeks of our arrival. We were devastated and upset, of course, but also scared beyond belief; where was the money going to come from now?

To add more stress, there was a recession and not a lot of work available. We had to step up, my husband had several jobs over a year or so, and then he set himself up in the maintenance business.

We got pregnant with our son, so this gave me time to take time out and qualify as an infant teacher, and we started to build our life back up. This life continued for a good few years, we absolutely loved our little family, and life was great. I felt more confident and good about myself, and the things myself and Ian had achieved. We adored our amazing little boy.

Then, out of the blue, he got sick, got rushed to A & E, and he got diagnosed with Type1 Diabetes. To say we were devastated was an understatement. The doctor said if we had left it any longer, bringing him in, we could have lost him. That day, our world changed forever. We had to step up, learn, and keep our son fit, healthy, and alive. Life was difficult, with three hourly checks at night, and not a lot of sleep was had! Learning about carbs, insulin, highs, lows, working out the insulin needed for eating meals, how other elements can contribute to the highs and lows, emotions, other illnesses, etc., and much, much more. My life was consumed by this. I immersed myself in finding out everything possible to keep him safe and healthy. But whilst doing this, I started back with extreme anxiety, sadness, and anger about everything, mostly about keeping our son safe. But I had to concentrate on our son. We learned to cope, and our son was and still is amazing. So life continued.

Then the world stopped!

Fast-forwarding through years of adapting to a new life, our son's diagnosis, and then lockdown happened! During the first few weeks, I felt lost and scared for the future, as did most people. But then I had time to relax, something I hadn't done for a long time, plus time to reflect.

The lockdown introduced a pivotal moment. We were stuck indoors right now, but we were lucky enough to have a beautiful sunny outside space, now I started to appreciate what we had and also what we could have.

After a few weeks of getting a new indoor routine going, an online opportunity flickered up on my social media feed—a chance to be an entrepreneur with minimal investment, flexible hours, and global reach. You get the picture. It completely opened my eyes. I hadn't even thought about working online. So I gave it a go, but unfortunately, after a few months, as you've probably guessed, this endeavour proved unsuccessful. Still, it planted a seed of hope within me, a realisation that there was an avenue where I could thrive online and maybe even be creative. It gave me the hope that there could be something out there for me, why not? It was like a light bulb moment for me, and it ignited a newfound determination to explore and work for myself. I could actually do this, I thought. So, the research and studying started, and to be honest, it still continues.

I studied and studied, invested in lots of courses, used my knowledge and experience of working with children and my creative skills, and produced my first children's learning book. I absolutely loved the creative process, from writing and designing the cover to producing the book itself. And it sold; I had the bug and truly started to believe I could do it. I continued to produce other books because I loved the process so much, busy working all day and producing at night. Yes, we had all gone back to work by then. But after a few months, it happened: hardly any sales, and the self-doubt set in; I was almost manifesting no sales, as I hadn't even told anyone, only my very close family. No advertising, no information on social media, nothing! And again, it started.

"I'm not good enough for this; why did I even think people would buy my books? How stupid am I to think I would be successful? This is ridiculous."

The self-sabotage and negative comments about my past way of life came back! Even greater, as I'd invested such a lot of my time. I felt stupid to have ever believed I could do it. Time went on, and I just ignored the books. It was another failed idea on my part, I thought!

I started to look for something else to fuel my creativity, and again, I searched and studied and came across a platform to produce and sell digital downloads. It was more to feed my need to be creative.

Using my teaching and creativity skills, another journey started! Again, I loved the creative process but never really told anyone and just continued producing items, no surprise to no avail in sales!

After a few months, I was feeling very low and deflated and in the zone of contempt; this is my life; I'm in my early fifties; this is my lot. Head down, work for someone else, the best I could achieve. Even though this is what I thought, deep down, I really still yearned for the freedom of being an entrepreneur. Fuelled by this desire, I continued scrolling the social networks, and my research led me to a new business platform; what is this all about, I thought? Out of curiosity, I signed up; I thought I would give it a go for a month and see what would happen. Well, this proved to be the best thing to have happened to me in a long time. It is an online haven for professionals and budding entrepreneurs. Here, I found resonance and understanding among peers who shared my aspirations. I was so buzzing to be around like-minded individuals that would help in any way they could—giving their expertise in an array of businesses.

Within this community, I also connected with an amazing woman, Amanda Brenkley, she is an exceptional coach, and healer, with an abundance of qualifications and knowledge. I felt such a connection with her from the beginning. She has influenced and reshaped my mindset through personalised sessions, hypnosis, coaching, and gratitude exercises. I started to believe I could achieve. And be truly grateful for what I already have.

Seeking guidance and support from mentors and a nurturing community has played a pivotal role in my journey. Their insights, encouragement, and unwavering support provided and still provide me with diverse perspectives and invaluable wisdom. Engaging with a supportive community has created a safe space, enabling me to challenge self-limiting beliefs and embrace my journey toward self-worth.

The Present

I've learned to embrace my imperfections and how to anchor myself in the present moment, liberating me from the clutches of past insecurities and future anxieties. It allows me to redirect my focus toward the journey rather than fixating on the destination, fostering a profound sense of self-awareness and appreciation for the progress I make daily. This community made me realise how much I have learned and achieved and made me recognise my accomplishments. And very importantly, it taught me how to be truly grateful.

Today, I proudly showcase several books on Amazon. I am the proud owner of an Etsy shop and am also at the beginning of my journey to be an Amazon seller. Amongst all this, I prioritise gratitude, acknowledging new blessings that unfold each day. I am by no means at the end of my entrepreneurial journey; I am truly at the beginning, with a full heart of gratitude and love for every minute of the journey. I have learnt to be truly proud of what I have achieved so far. My journey from battling self-doubt and imposter syndrome to establishing three online businesses has been transformative. Embracing vulnerability, learning from setbacks, and cultivating self-belief have been the cornerstones of my growth. The path hasn't been easy and is still challenging at times, but the lessons learnt and the confidence gained have been and continue to be invaluable. It is shaping me into a resilient person, unafraid to chase dreams and create meaningful change.

Thank you to everyone in my life who has made me realise that I can and will do this! If I can, you all can! Follow your heart's desire, it's never too late to change, go get em!

Linktree: www.linktr.ee/michellewynne85

CHAPTER 13

Sally Tarbox

Owner and CEO at The Empowerment Movement

Small Town Girl

I lay in bed on another hot summer's morning, the windows are open, but the curtains shut, and as I open my eyes, I wake to the sound of nothing but birds singing, the curtains waving in the breeze, and a sense of the cool air on my cheeks. I am 6 years old, full of fun and excitement for another hot summer's day.

I grew up with what on paper, seemed like the perfect middle-class nuclear family. Dad worked long hours and spent most of his weekends around the house carrying out various DIY tasks, and Mum was a teacher at a large school in town. We lived in a small country village where everyone knew everyone, and if you went out to play, you came home when it was dinner time.

I attended the local village school with classes no larger than 15 children, and although this life was nice, I found it extremely hard to fit in. Mum and Dad brought me and my sisters up in a strict church of England home and rarely interacted with neighbours, so local friends were few and far between. With sisters 7 and 10 years older than me, I found myself on my own a lot. As I grew up, although I loved my sisters dearly, I always felt inferior to them. To me, they were perfect, and somehow, I was not! Somehow, in my head, I developed a sense of feeling like I just wasn't good enough from an early age. As the years rolled on, I found two friends locally who I enjoyed being around, and their houses were always buzzing with people coming and going; the atmosphere was fun and vibrant, and with parents I could talk to and ask all those tricky questions a young girl would have, and who helped me fill the void of loneliness I had felt for many years.

By the age of 12, I found myself gone from being a small country girl to being sent to a senior school 10 miles away in the next biggest town, surrounded by people and situations I had never experienced before in my life. Coming from a school much further away, the sense of fitting in and being good enough became even harder. Most children had moved up naturally from local schools, so they had made friends and groups, and here I was, like a duck out of water.

Diets, Depression, and Despair

Sadly, by the age of 14, I had somehow found myself in a never-ending dark loop; the pressure was on within school, my sisters now had moved on, and although I had found my circle of friends, the wanting to fit in still haunted me.

I tackled with the same sense of never feeling good enough and fitting in through no more than control, control of what I put in my body, and within the space of a year, I had gone from a vibrant girl to one rattled with fear, anxiety, depression and an extremely dangerous eating disorder.

I worked hard for my grades, but with no one around me to talk to, I worked harder with how I looked. The more weight I lost, the more people spoke to me, and the better it made me feel. Lost and lonely in the middle of the night, I would sit on the side of my bed, fighting the thoughts within my head to get up and exercise again. It had got so extreme that my hair had begun to fall out, and my fingernails had fallen off. I had hit rock bottom, and the sense of being in control had ebbed away as I found myself being controlled by something much bigger: the thoughts within my mind.

Now, my mum is a lovely lady; she did all the things that a mum should do for their children, and although we were far from spoilt, we never went without. Sadly, though my mum wasn't a talker, some things were never spoken about, and deep emotional conversations were one of them. I know she found my teenage years nearly as hard as I did, and she never understood why I was struggling as much as I was mentally and physically. Any questions about what I was eating or why I wasn't eating nearly always resulted in an argument, and as the despair grew on both sides, the monster of anorexia only grew bigger. How would this cycle end?

Luckily, the universe had another plan for me, and by the time I was 16, I found myself being the local babysitter for other families within the village. I was back to being surrounded by other families I felt at home with. One family saw my pain and decided that it was time to talk. The mum was bright, loud, and vivacious; her energy filled the room, and you couldn't help but laugh and smile around her; she talked about everything and anything; nothing was ever off the table.

She and her husband were singers in a local band, so random babysitting soon turned into every weekend, and quickly, I found myself in their house more than my own.

I loved it; the energy she brought was like something I had never experienced before, and slowly, it started to rub off on me, it was like a drug, something you craved to be around, and with time, I found myself beginning to flourish like a tree in winter which had now felt the warmth of the spring sunshine, and that's where the internal healing had begun.

Rat Race to Relief

My university years passed quickly, and like so many other people, I found myself on the other side of a 3-year degree and thrown into a world where getting a 'good job' was the main goal. I did everything from running pubs and launching new businesses to working in IT sales. Soon enough, I found myself thrown into the depths of the corporate world, the money, the travel, the buzz I thrived off, but after eight years of hustling, I noticed that I had gone from loving it to loathing it. The questionable conversations and pressure to impress the right people was something that never felt right to me; the fact that someone else got to dictate how many days off a year I could take and what time I should start and finish all started to feel alien. I knew deep down I was a hard worker, and I could deliver, I would go above and beyond for my clients and colleagues so why was it ok for someone else to measure this on their scale?

Settled in London and working in IT I soon found myself at home after nearly eight months off work with a baby in my arms. My time to go back to work was looming like a dark cloud hanging over me. I sat on my sofa covered in the latest vegetable I had decided to puree, my house looking like a bunch of over-excited monkeys had stormed through, my beautiful daughter in my arms, and I burst into tears.

I loved her so dearly, but I didn't want to leave her, I didn't want to raise her to believe that she could be or do anything she wanted in life if I felt like my life wasn't the same, surely that would make me a fraud or a liar. With tears running down my face, I did something I will never forget, which was the catalyst to the start of something truly special.

After 45 minutes, I got off the phone with my very best friend. She is an amazing girl, strong, ambitious, a formidable force, a successful businesswoman, a mother, and almost always a 'fck YES' kind of girl. We had met in sixth form; her wit, humour, and drive for fun had always made me light up, and no matter the distance or time that had passed, it was always like nothing had changed. She was the kind of girl who, when covered in puree and tears running down your face, would pull you out of the trenches, dust you off, look you dead in the eye, and say......'Right, what's next? You want more; you need to go and get it.'

Getting off the phone, she gave me one person's name to look up online, someone who, in later years, I realised I had already met at a wedding of another friend of ours. This lady was making waves in the online space, she was a business coach, a mindset coach, and someone who believed everything to do with universal energy and manifestation....a world that to me was completely new.

It quickly became my new drug, my new high, thrown into a world where other women were lifting each other up, they were celebrating each other's success and cheering each other on from the sidelines. I joined every masterclass this coach had going. I would sit on my laptop every evening, laughing my socks off, listening to her next live, her next seminar, or talk. I started to learn about how energy works, how our internal world soon reflects our external, and how we are master manifesters, I started to understand my limiting beliefs and that slowly, I needed to heal that little girl inside of me who once deep down believed she was not good enough and not worthy enough but who had masked it for years in other ways.

Family & Freedom

Truth be told, I did end up back in the corporate world with my daughter in childcare, but something massive had changed inside of me. The desire to work the hours I wanted and set up something on my own had turned into a deep desire to give back to other people.

My mindset had completely developed; it had changed, and I was morphing into someone I had started to fall in love with again, and I wanted to be able to help other women do the same.

By the end of 2019, the world was changing into something we had never seen before, COVID was looming, and people were becoming frightened. As the world paused for some time, I took this as the biggest opportunity I could; now it was my time. A friend of mine has recently set up an Amazon business, so pointed me in that direction, and I took it on with both hands, knowing that even if this didn't work, the learnings I would take from it would aid me in every way. I would sit for days looking at trends of what people were buying or how they were buying whilst still dedicating time and space every day to keep my mindset healthy and growing.

Growing up in the countryside with over-excited labradors in the family home, I had always had a deep sense of love, compassion, and empathy for animals and the natural world around us. As I carried on with my research, I could see that the world was changing; people were becoming so much more aware of what they were putting in their bodies or on their bodies, and they were becoming aware of what they put on their children's bodies, and they were aware of what they were putting on their pets.

Our pets at home really do become part of the family; they are always there for us, a constant source of love and reassurance; they are our best friends, our confidants, and our loyal companions. With this in mind, the foundations of my brand quickly evolved, and from one product idea came a range of products. This is how Howl Natural was born, a completely natural range of pet products with no nasty chemicals in sight.

Howl Natural puts our pet's health back at the forefront as from personal experience, I knew that when our pets are ill or suffering, then it affects the whole family unit. We wouldn't bathe ourselves or our children in chemicals or words we had to decode online to understand, so why would we do it to our most loyal companions?

Excitedly, I took it to market. This was my brand, my passion, and I was doing it my way. I quickly found myself at shows and events and being asked to speak about the brand. The products were listed on major shopping platforms, stocked in retailers across the company, and shipped out globally. Did I make mistakes along the way.....of course, I did, some much bigger than others, but every single time, I learned to look at it as an opportunity to learn.

Inspire and Impact

The brand quickly took momentum, and I loved it; I loved everything about why I had started it: to create change, to get people talking, to encourage people to question the once simple decisions they had made. Even though my life was becoming busier than ever, I always made sure that I took time to pour back into myself, to deepen my learnings of who I was and what was holding me back each time I came across a mental block.

Within a year, my love for learning and my desire to create change had taken me down different paths; I gained certifications in hypnosis, NLP, life coaching, confidence coaching, and forgiveness coaching. I started to understand why we as humans make the decisions we do, and how our childhood greatly shapes our adult life, and how our subconscious mind greatly controls the actions we take. The more I learned, the more I put my learnings into action in my own life, the more I saw positive results, and the better I started to feel in every aspect of my life. My internal system was changing, and so was my external

During this time, a friend came to me, and they were having a tough time; life was throwing them curve ball after curve ball, they were desperately low, burnt out from their job and from the desire to please constantly, and had found themselves on the verge of quitting everything due to the pressure they were feeling. Standing there in their cold kitchen on an icy morning, they looked at me and said, 'How have you created so much change in your life, and yet mine is crumbling?'

I realised that over time, I had been so focused on what I had learned through experience and learning and a desire to create change in my own life I had built up a toolbox of skills, so I started to give them some of the tools I had learned

Within a few weeks, their mood started to lift; I could see a much stronger version of my friend starting to emerge. Their desire for change and taking back control of their life had become so strong that they were open to listening and putting into practice what I was teaching. After a few months, a completely new version of my friend stood before me, raving about how much better and in control they felt and how much I had helped them on this journey. It was at that moment I realised that there are so many of us out there like that, who quietly feel lost, confused, and have a desire for change but not knowing where to start and that I could help others along the path I had once walked. With that, The Empowerment Movement was created, where I now privately coach busy corporate mums to create more time and freedom in their lives whilst mastering their mindset.

While building the business, I took on a couple of coaches of my own as I knew if I wanted to serve others in the best way possible, then I needed people around me who were the next version of myself. At the back end of 2022, one of the coaches talked of an opportunity she had to work with a major TV brand in the States. They were running a segment the following year called Women Of Influence, and she was looking for women who might be interested. Without hesitation, I contacted her and put myself forward, and I was picked along with a few other incredible women I knew of in various industries.

Excitedly, in November of 2023, I packed up my suitcase and boarded a plane to Florida, and off I flew to appear on Fox TV to talk about the businesses I had created and why I was so passionate about what I do. I can remember sitting on the plane and reflecting on how far I had come not only in the last five years but also since that once small girl who had a deep-rooted belief she wasn't good enough and could never fit in was now embarking on an opportunity of a lifetime.

I had taken the time to work on myself from the inside out, to understand why all those years ago, the thoughts I had thought had taken me down some of the darkest roads of my life and how now my thoughts and subconscious beliefs had changed and been rewired so much and as a result so had my external reality.

The week I spent in Florida was like nothing else I had ever experienced. Spending time with the other women who were also due to be on Fox TV talking about their businesses and the obstacles in life they, too, had to work on and overcome was something truly inspiring. The energy was electric, all bouncing off each other, the enormous passion they had for their businesses and their incredible desire to help others shone through. It was one of the most incredible experiences of my life and something I will be so deeply grateful to my coach for creating and being there every step of the way. The friends I gained, the powerful stories I listened I will take with me for many years to come, all ordinary women who have at some point in their life had their backs against the wall but have made a bold choice to turn their pain into power and now pay it forward to help others create incredible lives too.

I now know that our lives are a bit like a movie script; we have the starring role, we are the writer, the producer, and the director, and if your life is not playing out the way you want it to, YOU can re-write the script. One of the main basic human needs is growth, for when we are not growing, our souls become constricted. That is why I urge every woman out there to see their true potential and how incredibly powerful they are. You have one life; this isn't a practice run, and this isn't the trailer to the BIG film.....this is your life, here and now, so make sure the movie of your life is playing out the way you want it to.

If you feel struck right now, wanting change but not knowing where to start, I ask you to ask yourself the following questions:

What do you not want in your life anymore?
What is important to you?
What does your ideal day look like?

How do you want to feel every single day?

By asking yourself these questions, they will start to show you what is important to you at a fundamental level and what it is that you want to achieve. I encourage every woman out there to do this. If you want to create a world that makes you the star of the movie and makes your dreams, goals, and desires a top priority, then I encourage you to reach out because 'If mumma ain't alright, then no one is alright'.

Website: www.theempowermentmovement.com
Email: info@theempowermentmovement.com
Facebook – SallyTarbox

> *"Turn your pain into power and surrender".*
> *Sally Tarbox*

CHAPTER 14

Lara Lee Caine

Self Love Life Coach

My journey of self-love to success with healing, empowerment and mindset shifts

I want to be a life coach

I'm Lara, a certified Life Coach, and I specialise in all things Self Love and Inner Healing. I have lived and breathed the journey of learning about self-love my whole life, and I truly believe it's why I'm here: to teach as many women as possible how to heal their conditioning and emotional wounds—teaching them how to love themselves by healing the relationship they have with themselves so they can then become the intentional creator of their lives rather than the victim of it. We all deserve to live magical lives full of miracles and free from fear, where we can create a life beyond our wildest dreams.

I know how it feels to be painfully shy, having little to no confidence or any self-esteem. I know how it feels to think you are undeserving with low self-worth. Growing up, I didn't know how to speak up for myself; I didn't know how to create healthy habits like setting strong boundaries for myself and worst of all, I didn't trust myself. Being painfully shy as a child made me a very easy target for being bullied at secondary school. The first two years were the worst, and I just remember being constantly picked on for not being "ugly" and so quiet. They knew they could easily upset me and that I wouldn't retaliate in any way. I felt completely powerless and spent most of my time trying to avoid drawing any attention to myself, desperately trying to disappear into the background or hide away in the sickbay, that's if I hadn't been lucky enough to convince my mum that day that I was poorly and needed to stay home.

In my late teens, I came across self-development books and instantly fell in love with this topic; with every book I devoured, I learnt something new about myself. In my early twenty's, I read the book Be Your Own Life Coach by Fiona Harrold, that's when I knew this is exactly what I want to do with my life… become a Life Coach! To be honest, I don't personally feel you can be a good life coach in your early twenties as you need to go live life first, go through some struggles, go on a few journeys, become wiser, heal, and deepen your own self-discovery.

At eighteen, I qualified as a Hairstylist. I then worked for a large American-based company for the next four years, but at the age of twenty-two, I broke my foot (on a night out!). I had a plaster cast and had to have three months of work, that's when the entrepreneurial bug first got me, and I decided not to return to the salon I had been working for, instead, I would rent a chair in a salon and be my own Boss!

Over the last twenty years of hairdressing, I have earned reasonably good money, but I never had any kind of business plan, financial plan or strategy to grow because I didn't have any knowledge about any of these things, which is not ideal if you want a successful business. Being a Hairstylist for over twenty years has given me a great foundation for coaching because I love working one-on-one with women, creating a safe space so they can talk about their problems, sharing stories and discussing whatever is on their minds. I understand women so well because of this; I feel what others feel on a deep level, have a strong natural intuition, and am a great listener.

The path to inner peace

Over the last twenty years, self-development and all things spiritual have been my passion; I have relentlessly studied in my spare time any book or audiobook I could get my hands on, also coming across different spiritual teachers to learn from. During this time, I have learnt to understand myself deeply and how to love myself by healing the relationship I have with myself, which really helped me break the pattern I had of choosing controlling men and toxic relationships. By doing so much internal healing on myself and with the support of coaches at different times in my life, I no longer need to numb out to avoid my feelings with unhealthy habits.

I've learned how to control my mind and choose my thoughts intentionally, to re-program my beliefs, and I've discovered the path to inner peace by going from victimhood to the creator of my life. I can now reframe negative experiences and find the blessings and the lessons in each experience; I have learned to feel deserving of all my heart's desires and can now happily speak up for myself because I have released my people-pleasing tendencies.

I value my time and energy; I protect my energy, and I now have healthy, strong boundaries for myself and with others. Above all, I trust myself, and I make my decisions from a place of love instead of fear... a very important life lesson right there!

On my fortieth birthday, my sister told me, "You have to train as a life coach. You are always talking about it; you need to do this!" it was now or never and the perfect time for me. The training took me two and a half years, in between juggling being a wife and mother, running a home and still hairdressing two days a week, but I was determined to finally accomplish my dream and be able to do my passion for my job. Training to be a life coach really helped me heal internally on a much deeper level than ever before, as you can't help others heal until you have healed yourself.

Having coaching to become a coach also helped me massively to free myself from the constant rollercoaster of painful emotions of my unexplained secondary infertility journey that I had been going through for the previous three years, and it helped me to understand the messages that my "infertility" had for me. Coaching then helped me navigate the year-long and very difficult adoption process that we embarked on before deciding that the unknown risks were too great for us as a family. This is why I am so passionate about coaching, self-development, healing, and all things metaphysical because I know how it feels to not feel good about yourself, to feel empty, powerless and unworthy, and I know the dramatic, incredible and transformational impact that coaching has on our internal world and in turn our lives.

This is why I wanted to start my business, I was born to do this, and I know all the difficult experiences and situations I have been through in my life were just qualifying me for the job I asked for, the most painful experiences that I've been through help me to understand and empathise with my clients on a much deeper level. What I love most about coaching is the transformation that I get to witness when I see the light come back on in my client's eyes after feeling lost or in pain. That is the part that makes my heart burst with happiness because I know the impact I have had on another woman's life.

There is always another mountain to climb!

When I finally qualified as a life coach, I was over the moon; finally, after twenty years of dreaming of doing this as my job, I could do so! What I hadn't really thought about whilst training for the previous two years was what happens next. At this moment, it dawned on me that once you reach the top of one mountain, there will be another mountain waiting for you to climb! Twenty years ago, when I first wanted to become a Life Coach, there really weren't many people doing it as a career; now, every man and his dog are calling themselves a Life Coach or some kind of Coach even if they have never even done a recognised coaching qualification.

If you are setting up a business now, it is probably going to be online, or at least that is where you will advertise yourself or your company. It hit me like a tonne of bricks, the enormity of what it involves setting up an online business like coaching! To start with, there is your website, your social media platforms (and they all work differently), creating content, branding, messaging, copywriting, and who is your avatar? (your ideal client). Sounds overwhelming, doesn't it!? It really is! To be honest, it's enough to put you off your passion and purpose, no matter how much you love what you do. All these different parts to setting up your business are careers in their own right, which you most likely won't know anything about unless one of them is your actual job. The other thing is when most people are getting their business off the ground; they don't have a big budget to throw at these things to get a professional to do it for them.

This is also the reason why a lot of small businesses will fail because a person will set up their business doing what they are excellent at, but then they will find themselves having to spend so much time and effort firstly learning about all these different aspects, then spending all their time juggling wearing all of the hats.

It's understandable why a lot of people then end up wanting to avoid working on their businesses because they are spending so much time doing tasks they don't enjoy rather than the skill that they love, which was the whole reason why they started their business in the first place.

A book I read as I was starting my business and one I can recommend is The E Myth by Michael E Gerber. This book walks you through the steps in life of a business, from entrepreneurial infancy to adolescent growing pains to the mature entrepreneurial perspective, the importance of creating strategies yourself at the beginning of your business so you can then teach others how you would like things done and outsource these jobs as your company grows so you have more time to focus on doing what you love.

The other thing I did when first setting up my business was join an online community; whatever your business is, their online campus of experts has you covered with step-by-step tutorials for so many different parts of business. For example, social media, branding, funnels, copywriting, coaching, network marketing, and so many multiple streams of income ideas, to mention just a few.

So this is how I started my business: I created my website (got clear on my niche, avatar, messaging and services), I started to work with clients getting testimonials to build my social proof, set up my social media platforms, I started creating content, joined an online learning community so I could learn about the new skills I would need, also being part of a community is an excellent support team for anyone setting up a business by themselves, and I have just kept taking the next step which normally involves pushing myself well and truly out of my comfort zone.

Rome wasn't built in a day

I must confess I haven't found it easy doing such a huge amount of continuous learning for the last four years and setting up a new business as I have done this in between being a busy mum, wife, running a home, working two days a week hairdressing, and also more recently having a very scary encounter with colon cancer (thankfully cancer free now) but that's another story. Over this time, though, I can reflect that I have had to make many mindset shifts to enable me to keep moving forward with my business. I would like to share with you the ones I feel have been most valuable to me in the hopes that whoever is reading this may find value in my words.

DO NOT COMPARE - your day one to someone else's year five; they too were once where you are now, and as the old saying goes, "Rome wasn't built in a day" If you are a coach, for example, social media loves to show you more of what you are interested in which means you will be shown lots of other coaches (who all look like they are absolutely crushing it!) Do not get sucked into comparisonitis just focus on being authentically you and just taking the next step forward.

RESISTANCE - this guy will show up every time you are about to follow your dreams (along with its best mate fear!) Do not worry; it is a natural response during times of change and whilst stepping out of your comfort zone. You will recognise it because it will manifest in ways such as self-doubt, fear of failure, fear of judgement from others or lack of motivation. Pursuing your dreams means venturing into unchartered territory, which can be extremely intimidating. Resistance is just trying to protect you from potential failure or disappointment. I have found the best way for me to overcome resistance is to **TAKE ACTION**; just keep taking that next baby step because even messy action is better than no action. You will only grow outside of your comfort zone, so take resistance as a good sign when it rears its head because it is showing you that you are challenging yourself and growing.

PUTTING OFF SHOWING UP UNTIL EVERYTHING IS PERFECT (AKA HIDING AWAY) - Everything will never be perfect, and perfectionism will hold you back in business in several ways. Fear of failure and making mistakes, procrastination, overemphasis on details, unrealistic expectations and difficulty delegating. I found from shifting my focus from seeking perfection to valuing my progress, learning from my mistakes, and acknowledging that imperfections often lead to creativity has helped me reframe wanting everything to be perfect.

SALES IS SPIRITUAL, NOT SLEAZY- View sales as spiritual instead of sleazy, and feeling this deep within will help you to become comfortable selling your services or products.

Having a spiritual approach to sales means focusing on being authentically you, wanting to be of service, building genuine connections and relationships, having integrity, and realising it is also an opportunity for personal growth. See sales as a chance to make a positive difference in the lives of others then selling can become a purposeful endeavour.

COURAGEOUS CONTENT CREATION- Unless you are an actual content creator, this is the one thing that can tip you over the edge and send you into complete overwhelm. I found creating content so scary initially, and I would say it froze me into inaction, but the only way to get confident at something and to become comfortable with doing it is to be courageous and do the damn thing! as this is the only way to build confidence. Be brave, but do not do anything that doesn't feel good to you or authentically you, and just talk about what you love, as this is what you are knowledgeable in. Also, just try to have fun with it!

Final destination

There is no destination. This is just a heads up in case you are feeling in a hurry to get there because every time we achieve a goal, we tend to then just move the goalposts again (I know I do). I have realised there is no ultimate endpoint, and why would you want there to be!?

The most important thing you can do is enjoy the journey you are on, as in life in general, embracing all the experiences whilst trying to have as much fun as possible while doing the do. It is so fabulous to learn lots of new skills and knowledge, to keep growing, to meet new people, to make connections and friendships and above all, to keep pushing yourself out of your comfort zone. Business and life, in general, are both dynamic and ever-evolving; as you grow and evolve, so too will your goals and priorities, which will lead you in new directions with new aspirations.

It is important for you to have clarity on your vision, goals, and intentions; otherwise, it is like driving a car without knowing where you are headed, but you can still keep an open mind where you are able to be flexible and open to taking detours where necessary.

I will continue to be a lifelong student because I love learning. Next, I plan to train in EFT, which stands for Emotional freedom technique (tapping) and IFS - Internal family systems. Both are very powerful tools that I can use to help my clients, adding to my coaching toolbox. I love what I do, and I want to be able to give my clients as much support as possible to allow the deepest transformation as I can.

Being a part of this book is also an incredibly exciting venture, and I'm looking forward to the whole experience and any opportunities that may come with it. I have also had a book of my own in my head for many years now that I have been wishing to create, and I finally think it is time for her to be brought to life!

This coming year, I have also already invested in some business coaching, which will begin in May; I'm so looking forward to seeing what I will learn and then be able to implement within my business. I am also making a big commitment to myself to show up on social media daily in some way, shape, or form to be seen and to be consistent. I know this is the only way it will get easier for me, and I know it will help build my audience as well building genuine connections, relationships and trust. Now I have to do it because I've written it here in black and white, so please feel free to hold me accountable and check up on me!

Above all, my number one goal, priority and mission in life is to help as many women as possible to learn to love themselves by healing the relationship they have with themselves so they can become the creators of their lives, learning how to co-create with the universe a life beyond their wildest dreams.

Find me on Facebook, LARA LEE CAINE

**GET IN TOUCH & BOOK YOUR FREE DISCOVERY CALL WITH ME
CHECK OUT MY WEBSITE FOR MORE INFO, FREEBIES & PACKAGES**

Website: www.laraleecoaching.com

Linktree: linktr.ee: laraleecoaching

CHAPTER 15

Beverley Storey

Network Marketing Business Leader, Holistic & Mindset Coach, Teacher and Healer of Life's Obstacles

Wallflower to social butterfly

Welcome to my chapter

If we haven't yet met, welcome to my world. Hi, I'm Beverley Storey. I am a business leader, Holistic & Mindset Coach, Teacher and healer of life's obstacles. I work with those that have a deep desire for change, to heal and live a better and healthier life in mind, body and soul.

I was born and raised in the heart of South Wales, in a small valley town that once, long ago, was a thriving mining community. The last mine closed in 1985, and I still have memories of seeing large buckets of coal journeying over a busy road from the mine on an overhead system to the mountaintop—a nostalgic reminder of the industry that echoed through the hills. My early days of growing up are of a village that was more than a place, it was a living community. Daily essentials, smiles and local news were exchanged throughout the local shops that made up the community.

My days were spent playing outside; I consider myself lucky that I had a beautiful open forest on my doorstep; it became my playground and laid the foundation for a lifelong love of nature and the great outdoors. When I wasn't outside playing, I either had my nose stuck in a book, or you would find me in the kitchen, the heart of the home, baking with my mother. I grew up as a shy, introverted girl who still has a love for nature, reading and cooking. I've Transformed into a positive, confident woman with a passion for helping you to transform, find the calm within yourself, navigate challenges, and strengthen your mindset to live your best life, free of the shackles and pain that life has dealt you.

As a child with an aversion to red meat, mealtimes nearly always seemed to end in tears by me!! It was a battle of wills between my parents and me. My parents wanted to instil in me that meat was good for me and would help me grow. I just didn't like the taste or the feel of meat in my mouth.

I was always being kept hostage at the dinner table and not allowed out or have a treat until I had cleaned my plate. To this day, I am a non-meat eater; I prefer vegetable dishes and fresh fruit and always opt for vegetarian dishes when eating out. This early aversion to meat, in retrospect, has helped shape the foundations of resilience and open communication, which is something that I have instilled in both my sons.

Holidays, days to the beach or a drive in the car became a family tradition that was enjoyed by all of us and was always treated as a treat, and it was always instilled into us how my father had worked hard to get us wherever it was we were going to, these were enjoyed as a family; I have a brother who is five years younger, or sometimes with our close family. Adventures that shaped our family narrative and routines were backdrops of daily life that has become a ritual that has anchored me to my life's journey and a subtle lesson in the importance of daily routines. This love for structure has carried me forward, giving me a foundation for focus and motivation in the face of life's unpredictable ebbs and flows, shaping the person that I've become.

"Embrace setbacks as stepping stones, savour traditions as anchors, and dance with diversity. In the tapestry of life, each thread weaves a story of strength and adaptability."

Unveiling of a wallflower

Entering Comprehensive School is a massive step; you are thrown from the cocoon of a primary school into a Lion's Den! I didn't just have the challenge of being shy, but boy, when the shyness disappeared, could I talk? No, it wasn't this that caused me distress. It was seeing for the first time how spiteful and unkind kids of my own age could be, especially the girls. Picture this: an 11-year-old girl with thick, red, frizzy hair and a face full of freckles didn't bode well did it. I became a target for bullies, who would shove me, kick me, dig me in the side as I walked by and whisper insulting words in my ear when the teachers weren't watching.

My father told me to dig them back and stand up for myself. Yes, it was easier said than done when all I wanted was to melt into the background, not draw attention to myself, and antagonise these bullies further. It didn't take me long though, to surround myself with friends, the strength in numbers soon made the bullies stop. They got bored with me and moved on to torment others.

In the classroom, I was quiet; I listened and did my work and anything I didn't understand, I wouldn't ask during class but would wait until the end and then ask the teacher. They were always great, taking five minutes out of their time to help me. At the school discos, I would watch from the sidelines – a typical wallflower, as my father laughingly dubbed me.

I soon became that typical teenage girl who found an interest in clothes and makeup and wanted to look nice. But these luxuries came at a cost that my parents couldn't afford, money was tight, and it didn't grow on trees. So, to finance my newfound interest, there was only one way to earn it: earn it myself! Babysitting for my next-door neighbour's children, and waitressing, firstly for a local catering company and later waitressing in a local pub. This was to be my first lesson in financial independence and the stepping-stone to a path of learning, personal growth and development.

Leaving college after a two-year catering course at the age of 18 marked the beginning of my full-time working adventure that was to shape my journey in ways I couldn't have anticipated. In just one week of leaving college, I found myself having my first-ever interview for a kitchen assistant job and the surprise of actually getting the job. Stepping into a busy kitchen environment after college was tough, I was working alongside women more than twice my age and the hours were long and hard. But I loved it, little did I know that this job would challenge and test the strength of my character. I found myself thrown into a world where respect was earned and not given freely; it was a challenge that cracked my shell of shyness, teaching me the art of effective communication and leadership. There were plenty of challenges, which became stepping stones rather than stumbling blocks.

At the age of 23, just a month before saying "I DO", I found myself managing my kitchen. Transitioning from assistant cook to Manager was relatively an easy transition; I already had a taste of the role in my previous kitchen. But just like a caterpillar emerging from its cocoon, I found myself like a butterfly more than ready to step up into this new role. I was embracing maturity with strength, resilience and a determination to succeed. I did; I had many happy years in that role before my first son made an appearance three years later.

Metamorphosis

Leaving the hectic world of catering at the age of 36 marked a significant shift in my life. After spending a good chunk of my years managing kitchens, I decided it was time for something different, something unknown.

In my mid-thirties, I unexpectedly found myself diving into the world of IT (Information Technology). It wasn't some grand plan; I went to night school to figure out This tech Stuff!! I needed a change that allowed me to balance my work and home life, especially with two boys now in the picture.

Exploring networking during the boy's early years, trying my hand at home parties, selling china and then health products added a bit of spice to this journey. But being the shy butterfly I was, I knew that to be successful, I either had to change or overcome my fears, so I put myself out there. I asked everyone I knew, from family, friends, mums & dads, to have a home party for me. I can remember them looking at me and saying are you going to be ok to do this? You won't cancel at the last minute! No, I will not cancel last minute on you, and YES, I am doing this! You see, I had already overcome one fear, and that fear was walking into a room full of strangers for my first business meet-up. Setting up a home party in friends'/families' houses was a piece of cake as I knew everyone; they never knew, though, that each time I did a party, my insides felt like Jelly.

Then, life threw another curveball my way. Child-minding! For three years, as my second son was growing up, I introduced child minding into our lives. Being home with my second son while my oldest was at school seemed like a no-brainer; he would get company through the day, and I got paid.

I had gone from managing the chaos of a working kitchen to throwing house parties to the simplicity of child minding. It was this period that taught me patience, the delicate art of nurturing, and how to find the balance in the everyday.

As the years rolled on, a new chapter opened up. With my youngest son starting school, I found myself in the world of office administration. Those nights spent at night school were, at that time, more about learning new skills and adapting to the growing world of digital technologies and survival than any grand career move. It was about adapting to the changing needs of the world we live in.

But life had one more unexpected turn: in 2008, my husband and I took a leap of faith. Leaving secure full-time jobs, we started a business selling, repairing, and hiring mountain bikes. It wasn't an easy transition, especially with my oldest son leaving school to join us. Working with family on a daily basis brought its own set of challenges and financial struggles, adding a layer of complexity.

My son's transition from school to work was a different story. He found it very difficult to adapt to being with us outside of home life. It took quite a while for him to find that happy balance between work and home. But once he found his balance and realised that he played a key part within the business, he grew in confidence and was absolutely incredible.

This chapter isn't about glamorous pivots or smooth transitions. It's about the raw, unfiltered reality of leaving a job that I loved to start a family business. Working alongside my husband and son was both rewarding and challenging. The financial strains were real, and there were moments when the weight of responsibility felt overwhelming. I learned the resilience required when building something from the ground up, the highs of family collaboration and the lows of financial uncertainty.

From the chaos of kitchens, the rollercoaster of entrepreneurship to the simplicity of childminding, and how each step has been a building block in my journey, shaping me for whatever comes next.

The storm of change

Navigating the ups and downs of our family business, life as it often does, threw its share of storms our way. The financial strains were real, and the art of juggling personal and business decision-making whilst still being mum felt at times like a weight weighing me down with no release.

Well, in 2015, the release came when life dealt me a particularly tough hand. The New Year kicked off with the usual resolutions and plans; it started off so innocently. Fast forward to October, and there I was, starring in my own hospital drama, having a blood transfusion. My body didn't exactly welcome this and did not throw up a shower of confetti to celebrate!! Little did I know, though, that this hospital stay was just the start. What followed has been a run of illnesses with an operation thrown in here and there along the way over the last few years. I felt as if my body had decided to test me and put me on a health rollercoaster, complete with dropping me from a high point and spinning me around way too fast.

As you can tell, I have moved through my health challenges with a touch of humour and the odd drama; it's just my way of looking for the positives instead of allowing it to pull me downwards.

Maybe you are reading this, and you've faced your own set of challenges, too; perhaps your story is similar to mine, or your story is still unfolding, and the twists, turns, and stumbling blocks are keeping you on your toes. I get it: life can be an unpredictable rollercoaster, complete with those highs & lows. But here's a secret I want to share with you — within every dip and turn, there's an opportunity to discover your own strength and re-write your own story.

You might be wondering why I'm sharing the chapters of my life with you. It's not about dwelling on the challenges but rather about illuminating the path to thriving beyond them; if you are unsure how to rise above your challenges, then this is where I have another twist to my story and my path, which I will share with you.

I found myself stepping back into Network marketing, starting a product-based business selling cleaning and homeware products. It was this business that fueled a catalyst of events where I found I had more than just a passion for connecting and helping others, but building a business I could be proud of, and I was so proud!! So again, there's a twist to my story; sadly, this business went into administration!! To say I was devastated is an understatement.

Did I throw my arms up in the air, shout, scream, and shed genuine tears? YES!! And I am not ashamed to say this, but I absolutely loved that business. So, take two, and a second opportunity was presented to me—an opportunity to partner with A Global Swedish Beauty Company. Yes, I definitely had reservations, but what was there to lose? This was just a vehicle to earn an income while helping others do the same. The best part, I wasn't going to be alone. My team followed me, and I stayed with my original team from my previous company, so I wasn't alone, and we were all on this adventure together. Throughout all my adventures, my husband has been there right at my side!!

What a journey we have had together! Remember I mentioned that stepping back into a network marketing business was the catalyst that fueled a series of events!! I've found myself on lots of great adventures, from overseas trips to stepping out on stage and speaking to a large audience. I became a top recruiter and have helped hundreds to do the same as me. Yes, you just read that correctly, me, the shy wallflower!!

The social butterfly

It was also around this time that I started opening up to my spiritual side and found myself on a journey of spiritual awakening. I realised that along my life path, I have had what I shall refer to as my sabotaging blocks! And boy, I had/still have quite a few. You see, there's a lot more to my story I haven't shared!! The story of a massive financial strain that I touched upon in chapter three.

Having all your money flowing into just one pot that has to be shared by three people, paying business and personal bills is bloody tough. It's even more challenging when tough times stop that flow to a trickle with an economy crash, my health conditions and those bills that are a necessity in life. So you start juggling things, but it only takes a matter of time before everything that's being juggled tumbles and falls down. It really was a very stressful time, and for the first time in my adult life, I had to ask family for handouts to help us through.

I remember one Christmas; I didn't even have the money to buy a box of chocolates, so once again, the family stepped in to help. Imagine giving your boys an I Owe You note on Christmas Day; well, that was my reality. It doesn't matter how old your children are; Christmas is a special family time. I know it's about being together and not the giving of gifts, but it broke my heart that Christmas. It took me a long time to let that memory go. Over time, we got through that struggle, but it's still left an imprint in my subconscious, and I think it's this block that has found me sabotaging my own earning potential. But...on a positive note, I've been guided through an unhealthy money mindset to a powerful positive shift.

I've never stopped learning, I've trained, I have gained certifications, and I've read many books. To me, it's the most powerful learning tool you can have in your hands, and of course, it led me to write a chapter in this book you have in your hands!! I've gone through self-healing and have finally found my happy place. I've found ME! The quest to find myself, my why, my true path in life has finally identified itself to me, all thanks to the universe and my spirit guides. This pull I have always had to help others has never lessened; it's grown stronger over the years.

Naturally, I've expanded into coaching; yes, I am also continuing with my network marketing business. I am on a quest to not only build a thriving network marketing business but also a thriving coaching business. I've stepped into my true self with, yes, a little fear and hesitation, but hey, that's a natural feeling; we all have these.

I want to help you find your true self as well as helping you to remove your sabotaging blocks and discovering your unique path with my transformative coaching. I am dedicated to helping you change and overcome the obstacles that are currently holding you back. Helping you on your journey with holistic well-being in mind, body and soul through mindset shifts and manifestation practices and help you harness the energy to rise and shine. To find your happy place to live a successful life. I will give you the tools that you can carry with you, always.

"Not all Storms come to disrupt your life; some come to clear your path."

Storms are meant to wake you up, to shake you so you can move forward. They will pass, and the rainbow will appear!!

Bev x

My gift to you: Download my free workbook
RISE AND SHINE: A 7-day Transformation Journey
A morning routine that will help you rise smiling each day that will set the tone with a day of positivity

Website: www.beverleystorey.com
Facebook: www.facebook.com/beverley.storey.5
Instagram: bev_storey

CHAPTER 16

Andrea Rainsford

Women Winning in Business

If You Tell Yourself: You Can or You Can't. That Is The Truth

As children, we do not have the limitations we put on ourselves as adults. We are simply us. If I told you, one of my favourite pastimes as a 2-year-old child was dashing into my parent's off-license in Small Heath in Birmingham, grabbing a bar of chocolate and sinking my teeth into it before anyone could take it off me. What would you think? That I was confident, cheeky, enterprising? Yes. That was me, a free spirit keeping my parents and grandparents on their toes.

My Nan was my person; she cared for me and my brother every day. She was our constant, the one person who was always there and who shaped me into who I am today. I had 13 years with her, 13 lovely years; however, those years were simply not enough. I was just not ready for her to leave me yet. I needed her. She had been there every day of my life, caring for me, looking after me. How could I cope without her?

But leave me she did; she hung on as long as she could, but Cancer had ravaged her body, and she had to leave. I remember that day as clear as a bell; I walked home from school each lunchtime to Nan. We had lunch, and I'd then walk home to her again at teatime when we shared a coffee and a biscuit or two. On this particular day, there were clouds in the sky, deep dark clouds, many cars outside the house, and the living room was full of people. I knew, I just knew, she had gone. Life was not the same without her. My person was gone.

My parents worked full-time; they left the house early and came home late. Nan was there for us. Now she was gone, and I was alone. Life changed. I changed. I was 13, and it was just me now; my role in the household changed: housework, cooking the meals, and walking the dog, with everything ready for when everyone came home from work and college. Woe be tied me if I did not have everything ready. My Mom was not known for her tolerance and patience. She worked hard, was tired, and jaded at the end of a working day. She relied on me to keep the house going.

Without Nan, I had no idea who I was. I lost my identity, I became withdrawn, I paled into the background, I was invisible. Never seen or heard. I would rush home from school each lunchtime and evening, walk the dog, cook the meals, and clean up, with no time for friends or after-school clubs. My childhood was over, they needed me to be an adult. They needed me to take over from Nan.

My grades at this time were average; my reports and my GCSEs were average. I was, well... pretty average. The cheeky, enterprising, mischievous child was gone, long gone.

I decided to stay on and do A levels. This was not a clever idea. I had lost my identity; I had no idea what I loved or even what I hated. I felt like a failure. My heart, mind, and soul did not believe I would succeed. Mindset is the most valuable tool we have. If we believe we can or cannot, that is the truth. I failed. No real surprise; after all, I had already decided I would fail. I felt like a failure and behaved like a failure, so I never put my all into it. Plus, I met a boy. A boy who saw me, who wanted to spend time with me, a boy who made me feel like I was alive again. A boy who became my world.

My parents needed me to join the workforce, and if the truth be told, they could not afford to send me to university, even though it was my dream. I had been offered a place on a business degree course, but all that was immaterial now. It was time for me to go out into the world.

The boy ended our relationship after six short months; I was needy. I needed him; I needed him to see me; I needed him to take care of me and love me. He needed fun. I was monitoring my weight, checking what I ate, and over-exercising all started here. I was not good enough. This was proof.

At the tender age of 18, I started my career in corporate business development; this was to be my trade of choice. I loved this life; I loved the attention, and I loved that, for the first time, I was good at something.

Being good at something is infectious, isn't it? Especially when you have not been good at anything at all. It can become a drug, the serotonin you feel from the praise, the adulation. It can be addictive. Can't it? Addicted I was. Work became my life, my whole life. Well, there was a little bit of time to kill myself in the gym! When I was not making myself sick from bulimia, I was killing myself on a cardio machine of some description.

I moved on to work for two other large global corporate companies, EY and Eversheds. I climbed the global B.D. Ladder: I made a difference. I landed multi-million-pound contracts. I landed contracts with Peugeot, Renault, BAA, 3i, Lloyds Development Capital, and Royal Bank of Scotland. I put together and led pitch teams. I was flying high and loving life, flying all over Europe. I even met the man of my dreams, and he asked me to marry him. Things could not have been better.

We went on our first-ever holiday together. I made the flight with little time to spare; I had been with my team working on a new pitch to Renault. I flew down the motorway with minutes to spare, him shaking his head at me that work was the drug that filled my veins. Always late for everything, work came first.

We returned from holiday, and I had a huge client meeting with Peugeot. Up the M6, I went to our Leeds office. I collapsed. Never to work again. Life changed forever. Life, experiences, and events change us and our mindset. Don't they?
We do not always come through these events unscathed.

Life changed forever

It always happens to someone else, doesn't it? The worst never happens to us, does it? Always someone else. Right? Wrong, sometimes it does happen to us.

I never returned to work; as I said, we spent many months getting to the core of what was wrong. I was lucky that I had private healthcare, and they finally found its underlying cause. A Neurologist called me into his office one day and said: "You'll never work again" I remember thinking, he is insane. Who let him in here? Is he even qualified?

Yes, he was qualified, and he did know what he was talking about, and I never did return to work in a corporate office, even to this day. What followed was the biggest fight I would ever have. A fight for me, my mind, body and soul. A fight that would take everything I had.

I was diagnosed with M.E. If, like me, you are reading this thinking that it is yuppy flu, so did I. I thought that it was a non-illness, that it was nothing. I dismissed it, dismissing it at my peril! I did everything I could to get back to work. I fought, and I gave everything I had. To no avail. I got married during this time. It was the happiest time of my life. It was such a tough day, though, physically, standing, talking, having no energy and my legs looking to give way at every turn. But get through it, I did, and we had the best time.

M.E. was my body's way of telling me it was struggling, that it was tired and needed a rest. I pushed on; pushing through was not conducive. One day in 2005, Ian, my new husband, came home and found me unconscious. I'd had a stroke. Not a small one, not a tiny one, not one you can bounce quickly from, but one that had taken the whole left side of my body; I could not wash, feed or toilet myself. Sh*t.

We all have dreams, ideas, and plans of how we think life will be, don't we? Of how we believe life will pan out. My dreams were gone in an instant.

I lay in my small hospital bed, feeling so alone, all alone in the world. The reality was I was not alone; I was surrounded by five older ladies, all with dementia, strokes, and broken limbs, all needing care and rehab to help them return home one day soon. We all had one thing in common, we could not walk, wash, or go to the toilet alone. I have been asked many times since then how I felt, how I got through the days, and how did I not despair and give up on life. The truth is, I didn't know how long my recovery would be; I always had one thing. Hope.

I believe we must have hope to move forward, we must have hope to live, and we must have hope to succeed. The one thing I did have was hope. Hope got me through. Maybe they will let me go home today, and maybe today will be the day I will walk again. I spent six months altogether in the hospital. I got to know the nurses by their first names, and the doctors would pop by for a coffee when they were passing. I was 32, and you could tell they felt sorry for me. The pitying looks, the touching of my hand, the extra hot chocolate in the middle of the night when I could not sleep. They all tried their upmost to make my time bearable.

It was around Christmas time in 2005 that one of the Doctors said to me, "You'll never walk again' Ian looked at me, and I looked at him. We exchanged a look; I said to Ian, "He doesn't know me, does he?" And that is when the fight started. Right then, that minute. **Mindset. Belief. Hope.**

When we are facing something mammoth, we need them in spades, don't we? The fact you are reading my chapter and that I have typed these words may well be giving you a sign that better things are to come. However, I do not have the words to tell you how hard this period of my life was.

I was unable to do anything, anything at all. I had spent months trying to learn how to do just one small thing for myself, to no avail. The years and months stretched ahead of me; the doctor told me I would never walk again. But, if you think you can or you can't, that is the truth, isn't it?

I had a team, the A team, to help bring me back to life. A team to help me find my way: a social worker, a physio, an O.T., carers, Ian, friends, family and of course Ebby., Ebby the cat, our fur child. We all planned to get me back to health. I told them I WOULD walk again. I am not sure they believed me. I told them I would achieve it; I could see it, feel it, and breathe it.

I would love to tell you it happened quickly. It didn't. I would love to tell you that the following year, I bounced back, and all was fine and dandy. It was not. But I always had hope and I always had determination. There were many days I gave up, so many of them. Days where I would cry, have tantrums, cry myself to sleep, refuse to see people, days where I would hate myself and my body. Days where I could not see a future. I didn't leave the house for many years; in total, I spent seven years in that hospital bed. I did start to go out for short periods after 2-3 years. The odd trip to the shops and the odd concert, we would get amazing seats. There had to be some rewards for being in a wheelchair! Life was starting to return.

I announced in 2009 that I was going back to university! Ian left the room.

A Journey of Changing Beliefs

In 2013, the week of my 40th birthday, I graduated with a degree in Computing Science. I walked with crutches into my Graduation ceremony. I walked any distance for the first time. The cheer that went up was deafening. I will never, ever forget it. So, what next? I conquered the degree, the one I thought I would never get. What now?

The thing was, I was not going back to work anytime soon. I had my degree; it had been hard, so much harder than I had ever thought possible. The tiredness, the tests, the exams and with such a poor memory due to a brain injury and a body that was not used to doing anything at all, it was a struggle.

However, I was approached by a few people in the months after my graduation; can you build me a website? Can you help me with my SEO? Can you help me get an online presence for my business? I had never planned on being a business owner; I loved corporate, the camaraderie, the atmosphere, and the Andrea I was in Corporate; could I possibly be brilliant on my own?

Business one: SEO Angel was born in 2014, the year after I graduated. I named her Angel as my clients told me I was an Angel. I made such a difference; I changed their businesses and their lives. I spent the majority of my time in bed. I ran my business from there. I did not see a client for the first few years; telephone calls and emails sufficed! Those were the days.

At what point did my mindset change?
At what point did my business become a success?

My business and mindset changed when I won my first award. I was nominated for a Woman Who Solopreneur award in 2018. I was nominated as a finalist by the judges, and I then had an interview day. This day would be the first time I had been out on my own for 13 years. Ian and the carers had always been with me everywhere I went. I travelled 30 minutes alone with my crutches to my first-ever award interview and first-ever face-to-face business meeting. The judges all cried as I told my story. I went on to win—my first award. Sandra Garlick MBE, Dave Sharpe, Jude Jennison, Nishi Meta and Karen Heap changed my life. I, in turn, changed my mindset.

The award gave me self-belief. I had no idea who I was coming back from the stroke; I did not recognise me; who was this woman in the mirror? Who was I now stuck with these crutches and wheelchair, reliant on others? I certainly wasn't the Andrea I knew before; she was taking a lot of getting used to.

Suddenly, like a bolt out of the blue, I believed in myself and my business and could do anything. SEO Angel, with me by her side, went from strength to strength. We won five awards, we helped hundreds of businesses with their online digital marketing presence, and I was retained by large corporates Clarion Events and Elite Exhibitions as their preferred SEO supplier. I worked on huge events, from The Classic Motor Show to Home and Garden, increasing their ticket sales and attendees through SEO.

In 2021, all events stopped. My clients and work disappeared overnight. Also, at this point, my parents were terminally ill, and my husband was made redundant.

I needed to resume my place as the main earner in the household whilst taking care of my parents five days a week. I had to produce a plan, and quickly! I needed to pay our bills, keep a roof over our heads and be a full-time carer.

There is nothing like having your back up against the wall to make you come out fighting. I mean, I had fought back from a stroke; I was learning to walk again (it had taken 13 years, but I was still trying to walk); I had started a business and created a profitable, successful business; I had built a network of thousands. I can do this, can't I?

I created a mastermind. A 12-step programme to teach everything I knew to create successful, visible online businesses that gain consistent income. I filled the first set of places; I filled the second set of places later that year. I created consistent income for my business using group products, working just two days a week.

In 2023, I knew it was time to return to my roots. Business two: Andrea Rainsford Creating Business Growth was also born. It was time to get back to what I was brilliant at Business Development; it was time to step into the shoes of the Andrea I once knew. I now teach via my sold-out services mastermind to other business owners; I teach how I created a successful, consistent income business working two days a week. There is a link in my linktree at the end of the chapter if you'd love to know more about my life-changing programme. SEO Angel is ten years old this year in 2024. The pride is immense. Writing this chapter has made me realise what I have achieved and what I have overcome.

What I want to leave you with as we near the end of my chapter is: Never ever doubt what you are capable of, never! Never lose hope, never lose belief, never tell yourself you can't! You Can.

Last year, in 2023, 10 years after walking into my graduation ceremony on crutches for the first time out of my wheelchair! I finally WALKED again WITHOUT AID. 18 years after the stroke, I walked, unaided, on my own, with my own two feet!

I cry every time I write about it. How did I do it? I was determined. Totally determined it would happen. My mind was made up, and I believed I could. I am not sure I will ever lose the excitement of walking down the road on my own in my walking boots, splashing around in the mud.

So, thank you for reading.

My parting words of my chapter to you: You are amazing, you are fabulous, you are incredible. Never doubt what you can achieve! The world is yours for the taking, simply believe.

Andrea xx

Andrea Rainsford – Women Winning in Business
Linktree: www.linktr.ee/andrearainsford

CHAPTER 17

Abbi Titley

Business Owner and Author

My journey to Entrepreneurial Empowerment against the odds

The Emergence of Horizons

Content with life's simple rhythm, the thought of owning a business was as distant as the stars. Yet, when the opportunity knocked, it was accompanied by hours of contemplation, a heart-to-heart with my future husband, and a whirlwind of emotions before I could muster the courage to embark on this unforeseen venture.

Let me introduce myself: Hi, I'm Abbi, the quintessential wallflower. My childhood was a mosaic of obedience and conformity, this was a stark contrast to my brother, the ever-charismatic soul who could effortlessly captivate a room. Under my father's disciplined gaze in our military household, I learned to follow orders without question, nurturing a life that was safe, predictable, and devoid of drama.

My twenties ushered in a career in policing – a bastion of security and respectability. Yet, despite the badge, I shied away from the frontline, finding solace in the shadows where the details were mine to manage. Was this inherent caution a product of nature or nurture? The answer eluded me, but it was undeniably me.

A twist of fate came when my supervisor, perceiving a potential in me I hadn't yet realised, recommended me for a promotion. Despite self-doubt, I stepped into this new role, each presentation and meeting a battle against my own nerves. This period was transformative, subtly reshaping my identity until I hardly recognised the confident professional reflected in my colleagues' eyes, it seemed so far from where I was.

As the years passed, my personal life painted a different picture. While my career flourished, a longing for love and family gnawed at me. Braving the world of dating was a leap out of my comfort zone, filled with the anxiety and excitement of blind dates and the constant internal debate of head versus heart. But, as fate would have it, a blind date, orchestrated by a friend led me to my "Mary Poppins"

This metaphor likens the situation with my husband to a memorable scene from the film "Mary Poppins." In the movie, the characters Jane and Michael Banks write a list of qualities they want in a new nanny. Their father, however, deems their requests impractical and discards the list in the fireplace. Miraculously, Mary Poppins arrives, embodying all the qualities they desire, but in a way they hadn't anticipated.

My husband is like Mary Poppins, an unexpected but perfect match for my needs and desires. While he might not always respond or act in the way I initially expect or want, he ultimately provides me with what I need, often in ways I hadn't considered. My husband's approach of rarely saying no, but he will guide me with what he believes is best, reflects the unexpected yet fulfilling nature of how Mary Poppins addressed the children's wishes. Just as Mary Poppins brought magic and wisdom in unexpected ways, my husband supports and cares for me, sometimes grounding me when necessary, much like how Mary Poppins subtly guided and cared for Jane and Michael in the film.

However, life's journey is complex. Postpartum struggles and a battle with my mental health followed the birth of my daughters, leading me to confront vulnerabilities I never knew I had. It was a journey of rediscovery, of piecing together the various shades of myself – from the shy, reserved child to the assertive professional.

Then, as if by destiny, a simple act of liking a post on Facebook spiralled into a conversation and an unexpected business proposition. Initially hesitant, my journey through mental health struggles had left me doubtful of my capabilities. Yet, with my husband's encouragement and the allure of discounted makeup, I found myself embarking on a new adventure in network marketing.

Starting my business in April 2020 was a leap into the unknown. It demanded visibility that contradicted my introverted nature, but I embraced it with a newfound determination. Personal development became my compass, guiding me to understand and appreciate my worth beyond the confines of societal expectations.

This venture wasn't just another fleeting interest; it was a commitment, a defiance of the "imposter syndrome" that often whispered doubts in my ear. Through ups and downs, I persevered, driven by a desire to redefine my aspirations and prove to myself that my dreams, no matter how late they bloomed, were valid and attainable.

My business, initially a means to enhance my external appearance, evolved into a journey of internal empowerment. It became a testament to my resilience, a reflection of my journey from a life of conformity to one of courage and self-belief. Now, I stand at a crossroads where my past, present, and future converge, ready to embrace whatever lies ahead with open arms and a heart full of dreams.

Emerging from the Shadows: The Quiet Transformation

In the tapestry of my early life, I was a silent observer, content in the background. My childhood echoed with the quietude of conformity. School, college, a stable job - I followed the scripted path laid before me, rarely deviating into the realms of the unknown. In stark contrast, my younger brother was the embodiment of exuberance, commanding attention with ease and humour, his confidence an alien concept to me.

Raised in a household anchored by the discipline of the armed forces, my father's career instilled in me a sense of unwavering obedience. Dreams were simple and unassuming: a quiet life, a family, a sense of contentment in the ordinary. This vision of life was undramatic, yet it filled me with a sense of purpose.

My twenties marked the beginning of my journey in policing - a career choice that offered security and respect. Yet, in this world of unwavering courage, I found myself gravitating towards roles away from the frontline, content with managing the intricacies behind the scenes.

The foundation of my work ethic was simple: dedication, a relentless drive to complete the task at hand, and a perpetual smile, irrespective of the challenges. Whether this disposition was ingrained by nature or nurture remained a mystery, but it was undeniably an integral part of my identity.

It was in my second role at the police call centre that my supervisor, perceiving potential I had yet to recognise in myself, nominated me for a promotion. At the time, the prospect of advancement seemed more of a financial opportunity than a personal triumph. Lacking self-confidence, I perceived this step as a risk-free endeavour - if unsuccessful, the comfort of my old role awaited me.

Thus, I embarked on a journey marked by internal battles. Standing before a room full of peers, my heart raced, and my stomach churned with anxiety. Presentations became ordeals, and documentation was a meticulous exercise in avoiding embarrassment.

Over six transformative years, I underwent a gradual metamorphosis so subtle it was almost imperceptible. It was only upon transitioning to a new role that the change became apparent. Colleagues now looked at me with respect and acceptance, acknowledging the growth I had struggled to see in myself. The fear of public speaking and confrontation had diminished, although the cautious proofreading of my work persisted as a humble reminder of my journey.

This growth was bittersweet, leaving me feeling somewhat alienated from the person I once was. The comfort zone I had so cherished, where I was simply 'quiet, shy Abbi,' felt distant now. My professional life flourished, and even now, my social media bios echo my workaholic nature. Yet, despite this contentment, a restlessness stirred within me, a longing for constant engagement and purpose. In this chapter of my life, the transformation was not just about career progression or confronting fears; it was about embracing the unfamiliar facets of my identity and learning to coexist with them. It was a story of emerging from the shadows, not with a resounding bang, but with a quiet, determined step into the light.

Braving the Heart's Journey from Shadows to Sunshine

As I entered my late 30s, a profound realisation dawned on me – my life, though successful in many aspects, harboured a gaping void that my career could not fill.

My lifelong dream was simple yet profound: to find love, settle down, and embrace the joys of family life. This yearning led me to a crossroads, one that demanded a departure from my well-trodden path of comfort and predictability.

The world of dating, with its intricate dance of vulnerability and hope, was as daunting as it was unfamiliar. Online profiles and blind dates became my new normal, each encounters a tightrope walk between showcasing my strengths and masking my insecurities. The uncertainty of this journey was a stark contrast to my professional life, where the stakes never seemed quite as high. In my career, I had nothing to lose; in love, everything seemed to hang in the balance.

I remember vividly the day my friend Kate proposed a blind date. The photograph of the man she showed me sparked a mixture of curiosity and apprehension. My past dating experiences had left me with a clear vision of what I wanted and what I didn't. Yet, this time was different; my heart and mind engaged in a relentless tug-of-war, leaving me in a state of confusion.

Despite the uncertainty, I took the plunge, driven by a deep-seated belief that love was worth the risk. This decision, born from a mix of courage and instinct, turned out to be the most rewarding of my life. It led me to my husband – my unexpected "Mary Poppins," who embodied everything I desired and more, often in ways I hadn't anticipated. He became my rock, my compass, guiding me through life's ups and downs with an unwavering sense of what was best for me, even when I was blind to it myself.

Our journey together brought into the world two beautiful daughters, each a bundle of joy, challenges, and endless learning. The experience of motherhood was a whirlwind of emotions – the highs of love and pride intertwined with the lows of exhaustion and despair. It was a rollercoaster that I, like many mothers, believed I could navigate seamlessly.

However, in January 2017, my world came crashing down. Despite having everything I had ever yearned for, a sense of unexplainable unhappiness enveloped me. The struggles of miscarriages, the demands of working while being pregnant, and the overwhelming responsibility of motherhood took their toll. I found myself at a breaking point, a shadow of the woman I once was, grappling with emotions that seemed to control me.

It took me two years to confront the truth – I was not in control, and I needed help. This realisation was a pivotal moment in my journey, a step as daunting as any I had faced in my professional life or in the realm of dating. It was a confrontation with my own vulnerability, a stark contrast to the confident persona I had displayed in my earlier years.

This period marked the beginning of a profound journey of self-discovery. It was a time to learn not just what I wanted from life, but what I needed – to find balance, to nurture my well-being, and to embrace the complexities of my identity. My husband stood by me, a pillar of strength and understanding, and my daughters, in their innocent wisdom, became inadvertent guides in this journey.

In sharing this story, my hope is not just to recount my experiences, but to offer a beacon of hope and understanding to others who may find themselves lost in similar struggles. It is a testament to the power of braving the heart's journey, of stepping out of the shadows and into the sunshine, where even the most daunting challenges can lead to a life of fulfilment and joy.

From Doubt to Empowerment the Unexpected Clicks

There's an old adage that everything happens for a reason, and in the grand tapestry of life, each piece eventually finds its place. My story reaffirms this belief in an almost serendipitous way.

FROM FEAR TO FLOURISH

For years, I was what you might call a 'Facebook stalker' - an onlooker in the vast digital world, silently scrolling through posts and pictures, never engaging, never leaving a trace of my presence.

Then, one seemingly ordinary day, I did something out of character – I clicked 'like' on a post shared by a friend of a friend. This small, almost insignificant action set in motion a chain of events that would steer my life in a new direction. A lady, a stranger to me until then, reached out with a simple message about a mascara I had liked. Her direct approach sparked my curiosity, and before I knew it, I had purchased the product. This interaction, which I initially treated as a mere courtesy, soon blossomed into regular conversations. They flowed effortlessly, bridging the gap between two strangers.

As we conversed, she presented an opportunity - "Would you like to do what I do?" At that point in my life, I was struggling with self-doubt, a phase I often referred to as my 'head falling off'. My immediate response was a reflexive 'No thanks'. Despite buying the mascara, I had not even used it. Makeup and social media ventures seemed like realms far beyond my comfort zone. My life at that moment was about seeking tranquillity, a quiet escape from challenges, with my family being my primary focus.

However, the threads of fate continued to weave their pattern. The conversations with her never ceased, and as time passed, my mindset began to shift. The idea of starting a business was still daunting, but the allure of discounted makeup caught my interest. Discussing this with my husband, whose support and level-headedness had always been my anchor, brought a new perspective. "What have you got to lose?" he encouraged. "Buy the kit, get the training. If it works, great; if not, you've got some quality makeup."

His confidence in me was the nudge I needed. After days of hesitation and wrestling with 'what ifs', I took the plunge. It was a familiar road, reminiscent of the moments in my career when I needed someone to believe in me until I could believe in myself. The risk was minimal - just a small sum of money - but the potential for personal growth was immense.

The community I became a part of through this venture was unlike anything I had experienced. They were unconcerned with my past struggles; their focus was on empowerment, upliftment, and validation. The support, training, and guidance I received were transformative. Within just two weeks, I had managed enough sales to cover the cost of the starter pack, now fondly known as the 'Ambassador Box'. The excitement I felt was unparalleled; the butterflies in my stomach were not just nerves, but harbingers of a newfound sense of worth and capability.

Witnessing the achievements of others in the business ignited a spark in me. It made me realise that I too, was capable of much more than I had ever given myself credit for. This venture pushed me to think outside the box, to envision a life that was not confined by my previous doubts and fears. It was a journey of rediscovery, of realising that I could build something unique, something that was entirely mine.

This chapter of my life is a testament to the power of small actions leading to significant changes. A simple click on social media, which seemed so trivial at the time, was the first step towards a journey of self-empowerment. It taught me an invaluable lesson - sometimes, the most unexpected paths lead to the most extraordinary destinations.

Unfolding Dreams: The Rise of an Unexpected Entrepreneur

In April 2020, amidst a world of uncertainty, I embarked on a venture that was as unexpected as it was transformative - my own business. The journey began not with a thunderous declaration, but with a quiet determination, fuelled by the support of friends and family who believed in me, even when I struggled to believe in myself.

Network marketing was a new realm for me, an uncharted territory that demanded not just understanding its mechanics but also embracing its potential. My initial challenge was to step into the limelight, a daunting task for someone who had always preferred the comfort of the background.

Yet, determined to succeed, I donned my metaphorical "big girl pants" and plunged into the world of social media, sharing my story with an openness that was both liberating and intimidating.

This journey was more than just about selling products; it was a journey of self-discovery. For too long, I had placed the needs and happiness of others before my own, often at the expense of my aspirations. But this venture offered a different narrative - one where my goals and dreams could take centre stage. I delved into self-help books and personal development resources, seeking to understand the intricacies of my personality and redefine my aspirations. This introspection led to a powerful realisation - that there was more to life than the dreams I had set in my 20s, and that I was worthy of pursuing them.

The path was not without its challenges. After an initial wave of success, there came a lull, a period of stagnation that tested my resolve. My husband jokingly referred to me as "faddy," a nod to my history of fleeting enthusiasms. But this time was different. Unlike the fitness DVDs that gathered dust or the half-read books, my business became a constant in my life, a project I could not and would not abandon.

Yes, there were months when everything clicked, when the products were in demand, and my confidence in selling them soared. Then there were times when doubts crept in, whispering that perhaps this was just a hobby, not a real business. These were the moments when the imposter syndrome reared its head, questioning my abilities and my potential.

But one of the most valuable lessons I learned through this journey was the power of perseverance. I am not a quitter. With each challenge, my resolve only strengthened, fuelled by the belief that I could achieve whatever I set my mind to, regardless of the odds or the opinions of others. My business, which began to enhance my external appearance, evolved into something much more profound - a tool for internal empowerment.

Now, this venture has given me a new dream, and a new vision of what I can achieve. It's no longer just about earning extra cash for the little things in life. It's about feeling good on the inside, about realising my worth and my capabilities. It's about understanding that the journey of an entrepreneur is not just about building a business but also about building oneself.

As I reflect on this journey, I see it as a testament to the power of overcoming fear, dreaming big and the importance of self-belief to flourish. It's a story of transformation from a shy individual to an empowered entrepreneur, a narrative that continues to unfold with each passing day. This is not just my business journey; it's the journey of unfolding dreams, a journey that has only just begun.

Abbi Titley
Linktree: Linktr.ee/AbbiTitley

CHAPTER 18

Sarah Knight

Skincare Brand Ambassador, Mentor & Coach

My Inspirational Story: From Sideline Business to Soulful Pursuit

My Journey of Self Discovery & Holistic Health

As I reflect on the journey that led me to where I am today, I remind myself of the spark that ignited my passion for holistic health and little did I know many years later, the start of my entrepreneurial journey. It all began when I was 15 years old when I found myself standing at a crossroads in my life. It was the moment when everything changed, and the flickering flames of self-discovery ignited within me. This pivotal moment came with a diagnosis of an autoimmune condition that shattered my world and left me questioning everything I thought I knew.

At 15 years old, I was a shy girl who wouldn't say boo to a goose. I didn't fit in at school and couldn't find my place; I was bullied and felt isolated and misunderstood. I avoided speaking up to anyone about this, including my parents, they had their stuff going on, so I felt - I didn't want to cause any upset, it's funny the beliefs you pick up in life. It was no wonder then really that I suffered a serious bout of tonsillitis, one in which I found myself in hospital. It was a scary time, this only got worse when following the illness, my body developed a rash that covered my entire body. At that time, it was unknown what this rash on my body was, however after numerous visits to doctors, hospitals, and test after test, the results revealed that my body was attacking itself, mistaking its cells as foreign invaders. I was told I had an autoimmune condition – Psoriasis. The news left me feeling scared and uncertain about what lay ahead.

The treatment process was awful, filled with countless doctor appointments, medications, and hospital stays. I felt like a guinea pig in a lab experiment. I felt unheard and invisible in the medical system.

I was told the way forward was conventional medicine. It was an isolating path, and I felt so scared. Over several years I found myself in hospital being applied with creams and lotions, drug after drug, but these would only serve to mask the condition, for it to only flare again some months later to another area of my body.

There had to be another way, and that is when my journey toward holistic health and self-discovery began. I became increasingly frustrated with conventional medicine's limited answers and treatment options that only addressed symptoms rather than root causes. Something deep within me yearned for more, for alternative methods that could nourish not just my physical body but also my mind and soul.

And so, with determination, I set out on a path less travelled. Years of exploration and experimentation followed as I researched everything about holistic health. Yoga mats became my sanctuary, meditation became my refuge, and herbal remedies became my allies. Through this journey of self-care practices and holistic approaches, I discovered the power they held in transforming not just my physical well-being but also unlocking a newfound sense of inner peace.

I realised that the key to this transformation lies in understanding that true healing goes beyond mere physicality; it encompasses all aspects of our being - mind, body, and soul. Holistic health recognises that we are interconnected beings; what affects one aspect inevitably ripples through to impact others as well.

As I dove deeper into this world of holistic healing modalities such as acupuncture, Ayurveda, energy work, and plant-based nutrition, an intense shift occurred within me. I found the more I nurtured myself holistically - through nourishing foods specific to support my unique body or engaging in practices like breathwork and meditation to calm anxiety, the more aligned and vibrant I felt, and it was through these alternative methods that I began to find some relief from the physical symptoms, which nourished my mind, body, and soul, and eventually healed 80% of the condition.

But this transformative journey was not without its challenges. I faced scepticism from those around me who questioned the efficacy of these alternative methods. Yet, every doubt and obstacle only fuelled my determination to uncover the truth and seek a blended approach to my health and well-being.

As I continued my transformative journey of holistic health and self-discovery to managing my autoimmune condition, one thing became increasingly clear: the importance of quality skincare. I had always been conscious that what we put into our body, was just as important as what we applied to our skin, but never fully appreciated just how much. With this newfound knowledge, it ignited a spark – to not only incorporate it into my self-care routine but to share its benefits with others.

The realisation ignited an entrepreneurial spark within me, sparking an idea of starting a sideline business, one that aligned with my values.

My transformative journey was just beginning, I knew that the flames of self-discovery would continue to burn bright within me. It was now about how I would build a business and whether it would be possible around my day job.

Inspired By Change: Releasing My Inner Potential

I had never considered building a sideline business before, although I had always been passionate about holistic health and wellness, I never imagined myself as an entrepreneur. However, the more I delved into the world of clean skincare and learned about the harmful ingredients present in many mainstream products, the more determined I became to have influence.

Starting a business is never easy, especially when it is outside your comfort zone. Doubts and challenges flooded my mind as I contemplated taking this leap. Would people be interested in clean skincare? Could I navigate the complexities of entrepreneurship with my day job, whilst still prioritising my health? These questions were in my thoughts, threatening to extinguish the spark that had been lit within me.
But then I reminded myself of all that I had overcome on my journey thus far. The frustrations with conventional medicine, and the yearning for alternative methods - these experiences had taught me resilience and perseverance. With this mindset firmly in place, I decided to merge my passion for holistic health, day job, and entrepreneurship. The first step was acquiring knowledge and expertise in clean skincare products. Through my research and conversations with experts in the field, I familiarised myself with ingredients to avoid and those that were safe for both our bodies and the environment. Armed with this knowledge, it became easier to find brands that shared similar values as mine.

After much research, I found a brand with similar values to mine, they were clean, green, were ethical, sustainable, and committed to empowering women. After learning about the founder, I was happy I could confidently vouch for the products. I was hooked, and I became an independent Ambassador in early 2021.

Drawing on my Psychology degree and a certification in Network Marketing, I recognised that there was a need to educate women about making conscious choices in beauty products, and so with this goal in mind, this became my 'why' for my sideline business.

I knew for this to work, my mindset would need to play a crucial role, so, armed with journals filled with dreams, plans, and time-blocking techniques, I set out to nurture my personal growth and resilience. Daily journaling allowed me to release fears and set intentions for each day. Goal setting helped me create a roadmap toward success, while reflection enabled me to learn from past experiences and grow further. I surrounded myself with like-minded individuals, which became a key part of my journey. Being part of communities that understood the challenges and shared the same drive for success provided me with the support and inspiration I needed to keep pushing forward.

But blending my passion for holistic health and clean skincare products as an entrepreneur with my profession as a Project Manager wasn't going to be an easy task. I would have to find ways to leverage both roles effectively. It was during the Spring of 2023 that a pivotal moment occurred, which took both my sideline business and my day job to a whole new level – a campaign opportunity to act as a social media influencer in my day job. It was during this workshop training that I had a lightbulb moment - I had not recognised previously the benefits of merging my day job and sideline business seamlessly, through this campaign made me realise that the skills and audience I would be building as a social influencer would only leverage my sideline business, additionally the creativity and entrepreneurial spirit nurtured in my sideline business could bring fresh, unique content to my social media platforms.

It just goes to show to grab opportunities, you never know where they may lead.

The Perfect Blend; Finding Synergy Between Day Job and a Sideline Business

From that moment on, I began to see the benefits and possibilities of how both could work together seamlessly, which, up until this point, I hadn't appreciated and recognised the benefits of being part of an established company provided me with stability, flexibility and resources that allowed me to dedicate time and effort toward further growing my sideline business.

Throughout my years working as a Project Manager, I have gained invaluable knowledge and skills in organisation, time management, and strategic planning. Little did I know at the time that these skills would prove valuable in building my sideline business. Furthermore, the knowledge and expertise I gained from my career in project management allowed me to approach my sideline business with a strategic mindset, set measurable goals, and implement efficient systems for growth. This combination of entrepreneurial spirit and professional acumen became a powerful force that drove my success.

As my side-line business grew, so did my confidence as an entrepreneur. I realised that my journey with holistic health had prepared me for this new endeavour in ways I couldn't have anticipated. The resilience I had developed while navigating setbacks with conventional medicine now served me well when faced with the challenges inherent in entrepreneurship.

Cultivating Mindset and Resilience

One of the daily practices I have adopted is journaling. By putting pen to paper, I can reflect on my experiences, set goals, and gain clarity on my vision. Journaling serves as a powerful tool for self-reflection and allows me to celebrate wins along the way, while also acknowledging areas where improvement is needed.

Goal setting is another integral part of my mindset cultivation practice. By setting clear goals that align with their values and aspirations, I can create a roadmap for success. These goals serve as a guidepost during times of uncertainty or doubt, reminding me of why I embarked on this journey in the first place.

Surrounding myself with like-minded individuals has also played a significant role in shaping my mindset. Success breeds success when you surround yourself with people who share your drive and ambition. I actively seek out communities where I can connect with other entrepreneurs.

However, cultivating a positive mindset does not mean avoiding setbacks or challenges altogether. It is during these times that resilience becomes paramount. The ability to bounce back from adversity is what separates those who succeed from those who give up.

Setbacks are inevitable, whether it's facing financial obstacles or dealing with unexpected roadblocks. But instead of surrendering to self-doubt or despair, I use resilience as fuel for my determination. I understand that setbacks are not failures but opportunities for growth and learning.

Overcoming Challenges and Embracing Resilience

Little did I know just how much my resilience would be tested when I was faced with a significant challenge in the Autumn of 2023; I noticed a small lump in my breast. After attending my GP, they referred me immediately to a breast clinic for tests. I would receive an appointment within two weeks. It was an agonising wait and one I didn't share with anyone; I didn't want to worry them. The results would take two weeks. I did tell my sister at this point, and she said not to worry; it might not be anything, but I knew. The day came, I remember it was a whirlwind of emotions, what if, and everything in between. It was confirmed I had breast cancer; a whirlwind of emotions engulfed me. Fear, uncertainty, and sadness consumed my every thought, but amidst the chaos was a glimmer of strength that flickered within me - a strength that I had cultivated over the years through nurturing a healthy mindset and, latterly building my sideline business, which instead of derailing my dreams or dampening my spirits, only fuelled my determination to continue. The years leading up to this moment had taught me invaluable lessons about resilience and the power of mindset. Through countless ups and downs in life, I had learned that setbacks were not roadblocks but mere detours on the path towards success.

One thing that became abundantly clear to me was that anything is possible if you believe in yourself and refuse to give in to self-doubt. And so, igniting the flame even stronger, I set out on a mission to make a difference by using this health challenge as my strength and determination to make a difference and to empower women.

Resilience has become my guiding light throughout my breast cancer treatment as I tap into my inner strength. Each chemotherapy session is not just about surviving but thriving amidst adversity. I have leaned on self-care practices - such as meditation, gentle exercise, and nourishing food - to nurture both body and soul during this challenging time.

But it wasn't just physical healing that fuelled my resilience; it was also my belief in what I stood for. The power of my mindset became even more evident as I turned setbacks into opportunities for personal growth. I reframed cancer not as an enemy but as a catalyst for change - an experience that would deepen my empathy and understanding for others facing challenges.

My ability to rise above fear and uncertainty serves as a powerful reminder that setbacks can be catalysts for personal transformation if we choose to embrace them.

Empowering Women: My Mission in Entrepreneurship

As my journey of self-discovery and entrepreneurship continues, I find myself driven by a deep desire to empower women to make conscious choices in beauty products that align with their values.

I understand that empowering women as informed consumers goes beyond simply providing product recommendations. It requires comprehensive information about ingredients, manufacturing processes, and ethical sourcing. I have made it my goal to become an expert in these areas, diving deep into research and reaching out to industry professionals who share this passion.

With my knowledge, I intend to break down complex scientific jargon into accessible language so, that every woman can understand what goes into the products they put on their body. By providing this knowledge, I empower women to make choices that promote not only personal well-being but also environmental sustainability.

To further get this message out there, I have built an online community where women can come together to discuss topics like natural skincare routines and general self-care practices. These gatherings create an environment where like-minded individuals can connect on their transformative journeys. As my mission in entrepreneurship evolves, I become increasingly aware of the need to redefine beauty standards and understand that true beauty lies in embracing one's uniqueness and rejecting societal norms that perpetuate unrealistic ideals.

The Power of Transformation

The power of transformation lies not only in our ability to overcome challenges but also in our capacity to inspire others. By sharing my chapter, I hope to ignite an enterprising spirit within every woman who crosses my path. I want them to see that they too, could create a life of soulful purpose and impact, regardless of their circumstances or past experiences.

The transformative journey is an ongoing one; it is a lifelong pursuit filled with difficulties, triumphs, and setbacks. But it is precisely through these experiences that we uncover our true potential and find meaning in our lives.

I encourage you, dear reader, to embark on your transformative journey. Embrace your unique gifts, cultivate a positive mindset, and empower those around you. Through your growth and empowerment, you will inspire others to do the same.

In closing this chapter, I want to express my gratitude for reading my journey. May you always remember the power of transformation that lies within you, and may you use it to create a life filled with purpose, joy, and soulful meaning.

To learn more about how we can partner and build connections, connect with me on the link below

Linktree: www.linktr.ee/sarah.knight

CHAPTER 19

Sandra Fletcher

Wellness Coach/Motivational speaker

This is me

Hi, my name is Sandra, Sandra Fletcher. I am currently working as a Community Mental Health Nurse in my hometown, Greenock, Scotland. I live in a two-bed semi-detached house with my 19-year-old son Jason, our parrot Fletch and adorable dog Pat. I am in the process of setting up a Life/wellness coaching business; this is something I have dreamed about for many years but never had the confidence to do.

Where it all began

I came into this world in 1965, much to my dad's delight, after having two boys, I am the youngest of three. We lived in a 2-bed council house at first. My hometown Greenock, is on the West Coast of Scotland. Growing up I had the pleasure of two parents both working hard for all we had, I also had an aunt who was my godmother who spoiled me. I was surrounded by family who all had a decent work ethic. I was a bit of a handful. My mum, to this day will say worse than ten boys.

As a child, I was extremely fortunate with the summer holidays, and we rented a small cottage on a small island off the West Coast of Scotland called Millport! We went there for our summer holidays every year during the whole month of August. My maternal grandmother and her sister, Aunt Jessie, took my two brothers over to the accommodations and stayed with us for the whole month. My mum and dad would come over at the weekends when they were off work, they also took some time off. I was up nearly every morning to go to the stables and help get the horses ready for their 1st pony treck of the day, how wonderful these days were for us. This was where I started my love of horses and my work ethic. I remember leading the ponies along the beach; we would get free rides at the end of the day.

All my childhood years have nothing but happy memories. I started my world of work at 13, I had a paper round and worked in a fruit and veg shop on a Saturday, As I grew up into my early teens, I was a bit of a feisty free spirit! My mum would call it "wild" " She said she would rather raise ten boys! I spent lots of time in Essex where my godmother lived. I would go to their salmon factory and help, and most afternoons were spent at their friends' stables, where I would help and get to ride too. I class myself as being very privileged to experience all this at an early age,

My early school days consisted of me attending and then leaving to play truant at my friend's house. This was, I would imagine, a tough time for my parents as I, by my admission, went off the rails. I was not interested in school despite being clever; I never put this to good use, In the third year, I contracted Pneumonia and non-active TB. I was off school most of that year, and in hospital for three months, my parents were told, "If you have never spoiled her before, you should now". Basically, they were not sure if I would pull through. I left school at the age of sixteen; I could not wait to get out. I secured myself a youth training scheme that lasted for approximately one year, and I loved it, it made me feel all grown up. I then went on to work in an amazing salon where I met some great people who I am still friends with to this day. This is where my entrepreneurial love began; the salon I worked in also sold hair care products, and this is where I came into my own, I was the top seller of the products. As juniors we were on commission, and this gave me a taste of what it would be like to earn money selling products. The hairdressing salon I worked in participated in and hosted hair shows, which we all took part in, and hosted hair shows. It was a wonderful place to work, and this taught me about discipline at work.

The late teen years

At 16, I had my first committed relationship, I was head over heels crazy about this person, he was a few years older than me, and he rode a motorbike, I can remember this being an exciting time in my life. We would go camping with the bike to places like Fort William, a lovely place up in the north of Scotland, and various other scenic places in Scotland. We went on to be engaged. We were also planning a wedding, however I discovered this man was not satisfied with one girlfriend, he had lots of others that he went with behind my back. We went on and off for some time, and then my Aunt Joy set me up with a job and a room in her friend's hair salon in Jersey Channel Islands. I then secured my accommodation and a new job; I managed a hair salon. I was only twenty-one at the time, and this job gave me further experience in a managerial post and an insight into what it was like to run a business. It also further encouraged my decent work ethic.

I pride myself on moving to various places to live, which made me more worldly. I returned from Jersey and stayed in my hometown for a week or two. One of my best friends was getting married in a place called Slough, and I went for a fitting of a bridesmaid dress and stayed for over five years. I was in a new relationship, and we made Slough our home for five years; jobs were aplenty. I worked in various kinds of jobs, including Windsor Safari Park. Again, I managed different establishments, thus further increasing my skills and giving me a taste of what it would be like to run a business once again. Up to this time in my life, I would describe myself by nature as a "fixer", always ready and waiting to fix someone or something; I was always ready and waiting to help anyone with problems that needed fixing.

As far back as I can remember, I wanted to help anyone who was down on their luck, was bullied, or just needed to vent. This was the time when I discovered I wanted to have my own life coaching business helping others. I always believed in the past and that this was something I would not be able to achieve. I did not think that someone with my background would be good enough to be a life coach. After five years, I decided to come home to Greenock. I was still in the relationship that started in Slough, and we would be married; alas, this was not to be, as he called off the wedding six weeks before we were due to marry. When I moved back to Scotland, I lived at my paternal grandmother's house as she was never there. She spent most of her time in Canada with my aunt and her daughter. We were going to reside here until we saved up a deposit for our own home. Also, at this time, I had my first pet, a German Shepherd. I always wanted this breed of animal; however, when I lived at home, my mom would never allow it, although, as a family, we always had dogs.

When that relationship ended once again, my confidence took a huge blow and left me doubting my abilities. I was beginning to see a pattern with regard to relationships. I always picked men who were not good for me and did not have my best interests at heart. Once again, I believe I entered into these relationships as I thought I could fix these men and live happily ever after. I've always been a dreamer when it comes to relationships. I suppose in my mind, I was always expecting a happy home with children, a small cottage with a white picket fence.

Starting my first business

Around the age of twenty-nine, I attended a wedding in Essex. My cousin Kimberly was getting married, and my aunt, who was my godmother, had been diagnosed with terminal cancer. She was able to assist with all the planning of the wedding, which Mas held in their large back garden. The decor was unique. The marquees and gardens were all decked out with balloon décor; I thought to myself, this is the type of decor that was going to be a huge hit in the wedding industry.

As soon as I got home, I started researching balloon decor and found the company and Hillington. She offered training courses, It was a fabulous experience to train with the renowned Janey Bacon. I believe she was the person who brought balloons to Scotland. Her company, Balloons around Scotland, had some of the largest contracts in Scotland. I felt very privileged to be asked to assist with Glasgow Rangers end of end-of-season dances over a few years. This business was successful for several years. I collaborated with the biggest caterer in Inverclyde, doing all their functions décor. I had all the big local contracts as there was no competition. I continued to do my home help job for our local council. I can see now that I was still reluctant to trust my abilities to give up the job to focus more on the business. My mum was my partner in the balloon business. We had some laughs working together. It was a wonderful experience.

I was in another relationship, which I felt was quite serious; however, the partner at the time felt quite different as he was very reluctant to commit fully. Once again, I began to question myself. I had another failed relationship, and as usual, I blamed myself; in hindsight, I can look back now and see even then, I was a bit of a free spirit; I have always been fiercely independent. I like to earn my own money. My oldest brother and I were remarkably close. He worked as a disc jockey in all the clubs. This time in my life was amazing. I worked hard, and I also partied hard. I have always been extremely outgoing. I love to dance and socialise with my friends. My business was flourishing, and due to still working at my job around events, I was in a good place emotionally and financially. Everything went on as before. Over the next few years, I focused on my business and my job.

My late thirties saw me caring for my gran, running my business, and having fun. I took a trip to Amsterdam with my cousin and her husband. I met the man I went on to marry, he was English. We met in Essex in April, he moved to Scotland, and that July, we got engaged in September, and we were married the following April; the old saying marry in haste, repent at leisure is a true saying. After we were married, I became pregnant quite quickly; however, sadly, we lost this baby, which devastated me. All I ever wanted was a little boy with blonde hair and blue eyes. I went on to fall pregnant again. I was still managing my balloon business while pregnant and also having my full-time job.

We acquired premises for the business, and my mother minded the shop while I was at work; as mentioned before, I was feeling quite restless in this role as a respite officer. I started to think about other career options; I was in my early forties, and I have always worked for the past 19 years in elderly care predominantly. I also had the privilege of working with some young adults with learning disabilities as well. This was when I started to think about going down the road of nursing; I knew that I could never do general nursing. I was never one for blood and gore, shall we say.

My university days

In 2009, I applied to go to university to do a mental health nursing degree. This took me out of my comfort zone. I managed to secure a weekend contract and the respite unit I worked at. It was seven days a week for the next three years. Being at university was most probably one of the most memorable things I have ever done. No one in my family had ever been to university at that point. As soon as I began university, I knew I would have to hit the ground running, age was not on my side, so I could not risk failure, I got my head down and was laser-focused on all my assignments. I completed my mental health nursing degree in 2012, a BSc with a Distinction. While at university, I got the opportunity to study in a place called Lieria in Portugal.

I went to university there, and we were all split into groups as there were seven different countries there. Our task was to work together in groups from different countries to create a gold standard of how to nurse the elderly and a multicultural society; that was one of my proudest moments. My first nursing post was in a nursing home, which I hated! We had access to a program with the NHS where we got a part-time post two times 22.5 hours, one on a ward and the other in the community. Around this time, I did not have any small businesses, this was due to the number of hours I was working as a mental health nurse. It was still glaringly apparent that mental health nursing was the right path for me at that time. I still always had my dream of starting my own business delivering care of some sort to the wider population, and once again, I was working two jobs as the part-time role was not a big enough income. I joined the nursing bank and picked up shifts to top up my income.

Single mum life

I became a single parent with no other financial help other than my mum, and my brother Jason's dad has given tiny amounts over the last few years but nowhere near enough to keep a teenager! Most would never have guessed I fell apart! I had to get on with it as I was all Jason had to provide for him! Initially, I was in a financial mess!!! Days I could not afford a loaf of bread or milk!! Do not get me wrong, my mum and brother were always there to bail me out, and for that, I will be eternally grateful! Jason's godparents were also good to him. As the months went on, I sold Aloe Vera products and made tiny amounts! I worked shifts at the weekend and worked my full-time job too! I could not work any more hours than I was working; I was doing my best to sell as much Aloe Vera as I could, but it was still not enough! I had a higher mortgage, a car to pay, and had to put food on the table.

I have gained valuable experience in business, learning from historical choices that may not have yielded the expected results but rewarded me in the development of my abilities. While exploring the much-hyped crypto space helped me further develop my skills to identify risk and create personalised strategies to help me minimise risk and potentially lucrative but volatile opportunities. This experience was invaluable and taught me that not all recommendations are as straightforward as they seem and that a good practical analysis combined with tailor-made strategies for each uncertainty is fundamental to increasing the opportunity for success in my venture.

I was good friends with my trainer Emma; she was instrumental in me starting to believe in myself and helped me to address my lack of self-worth and confidence. I was self-conscious about my weight, and she helped me to start eating clean and taking better care of myself; in fact, we are going to be building my wellness coaching into her plans for her gym members. For this, I will be eternally grateful. Thank you also to my close friends and family for believing in me when I didn't believe in myself. I also met a lovely man in October 2022 who helped me realise that my dreams could come true; somehow, he was in the right place at the right time for me, and he believed in me and my abilities and to be a better version of me!

In summary, I have been in business for myself for over 20 years. All this experience has led me to where I am now. My journey in business has found me supported by some amazing people who have been instrumental in leading me to the path I am on now. I have always believed that things happen for a reason. Strangely enough, all my previous experience was preparing me for the exciting road ahead. If you are thinking of starting a business, do it now!

Connect with me:

Facebook: Sandra Fletcher

ACKNOWLEDGEMENT

In heartfelt appreciation, I extend my deepest gratitude to the incredible individuals who have played an instrumental role in bringing this book to life. To the badass women featured within these pages, both those who bravely shared their transformative stories and those tirelessly changing lives beyond the confines of this book – your courage and belief in yourselves and in me have made this journey truly extraordinary. I wish each of you boundless success, for it is well-deserved.

A special acknowledgment is reserved for Tracey Munro, whose invaluable book coaching played a pivotal role in birthing this work into reality. Tracey, your professionalism, and friendship have been a guiding force, and I am grateful for your unwavering support.

To my cherished family and friends, you are the pillars of strength that remind me daily of the wealth in my life. My incredible children, your patience, understanding, and unwavering support have been my anchors throughout this journey. I cannot express enough how much I value and love you both.

To my beloved grandparents, Ann and Martin, who have assumed the mantle of parenting with unparalleled grace and love – you are my role models and steadfast support. The depth of my gratitude and love for you both is immeasurable.

A heartfelt thank you to my sister Gemma, whose had resilience and patience over the years with all my numerous entrepreneurial ideas and constant woohoo ideology, you have been a constant source of inspiration. Your support and understanding have been a beacon of light on this creative journey. We have always been there for each other and always will. Mum will be proud of us both!

I am certain that the universe conspired to bring these remarkable individuals into my life. No combination of words can adequately convey the depth of my gratitude to all who believed in me. This book stands as a testament to the collective strength of a supportive community, and I am blessed to have each of you in my life.

Amanda x

Supporting Macmillan Cancer Support
Scan the QR code to Join us on Facebook

Printed in Great Britain
by Amazon